LET THEM TALK LET ME BUILD

The 60-Day Boundary-Setting Workbook for

People-Pleasing Recovery

Stop caring what they think and start creating the life you want

Addison Gray

YOUR GIFT FOR THE JOURNEY

Let Me Build Power Toolkit - Your 60-Day Companion Tools

Dear friend,

While writing this book, I designed it so you could practice everything without needing additional materials. However, from personal experience and reader feedback, I've learned that having specific support tools makes the 60-day journey more manageable and effective.

*That's why I created the **Let Me Build Power Toolkit.***

What's Inside The Toolkit?

√ **Quick-Start Toolkit**

- *Detailed checklist for your first 7 days*
- *Know exactly what to do each day, no guesswork needed*

√ **30 Morning Affirmations**

- *30 power affirmations designed for the 4 stages*
- *Print as 7x10cm cards or save on your phone*
- *One each morning, as a reminder of your inner strength*

√ **12 Ready-to-Use Boundary Scripts**

- *4 scripts for work situations*
- *4 scripts for family relationships*
- *4 scripts for social circumstances*
- *Pre-written, just adjust to fit your needs*

√ **Troubleshooting Guide**

- *What to do when you want to quit*
- *How to handle unsupportive loved ones*
- *Overcoming the "I'm progressing too slowly" feeling*

√ **Printable Resources**

- *A3 Timeline Poster to track your progress*
- *A6 Values Compass Card - carry your core values with you*
- *Completion Certificate - celebrate finishing your journey*

Get Your Free Power Toolkit

ACCESS IN SECONDS:

SCAN QR CODE **or VISIT:** *https://bit.ly/letmebuildtoolkit*

This Power Toolkit is completely free for readers, helping you apply the exercises in your 60-day journey effectively and systematically.

A Note From Me

This toolkit isn't a marketing gimmick or add-on. These are tools I genuinely believe will support your transformation journey.

Think of it as a companion - always there when you need a reminder, encouragement, or specific guidance.

I hope you'll use these tools to make the next 60 days the beginning of a life lived on your own terms.

"While they exhaust themselves judging, you'll be busy building - with the right tools in hand."

INTRODUCTION

Opening Message

"Maybe your garden isn't growing BECAUSE every time the flowers start to bloom, you cut them to prove to someone else that you're a Gardener."

Welcome to your 60-day transformation journey.

Each day, how much mental energy do you waste worrying about what others think? This isn't a rhetorical question. In a world of perfect Instagram feeds, viral TikToks, and constant pressure to succeed, our minds are hijacked by questions like:
"Are they judging my career choices?"
"If I don't respond to that email at 11 PM, will they think I'm lazy?"
"Should I post this, or will people think I'm showing off?"

Meanwhile, our actual dreams, talents, and potential sit on the back burner, waiting to be nurtured.

This book begins with a simple truth: **You can't control what others think. But you absolutely can control how much it affects you.**

The Core "Let Them" Philosophy

"Let Them Talk, Let Me Build" isn't a new philosophy. It's an ancient truth reimagined for modern society – a society where opinions, comments, and judgments bombard us from every direction, every platform, every screen.

Let's be clear: *"Let Them"* isn't about silence or giving up. *"Let Them"* isn't about surrendering your voice or your dreams. "Let Them" isn't about retreating from life.

"Let Them" is precisely:

Deeply understanding that others' reactions aren't about you – they're about them

Recognizing that others' opinions are projections from their inner world

Redirecting energy from *"worrying what others think"* to *"building your own life"*

When you *"Let Them Talk,"* you're applying a powerful truth: *"Nothing others do is because of you. What they say and do is a projection of their own reality."* You learn to become immune to others' opinions – not by becoming callous, but by recognizing your worth doesn't depend on external validation.

And when you *"Let Me Build,"* you redirect that energy – energy previously consumed by worry, reactivity, and proving yourself – into creating the life, values, and achievements that truly matter to YOU.

Your 60-Day
Self-Building Commitment

Before beginning this journey, I invite you to make a commitment to yourself. Not to me. Not to others. To YOU.

> **Note:** This commitment isn't a chain. It's a compass. When you feel lost, come back here to find your direction. And if you have a less-than-perfect day, don't worry. Just start again tomorrow. The power of this process lies in persistence, not perfection.

Personal Commitment Statement

I, ________, commit to the next 60 days of building myself. I understand that on this journey, I will:

- Face uncomfortable truths about how I've let others' opinions shape my life

- Release the need for universal approval and acceptance

- Become the gatekeeper of my energy and attention

- Create new boundaries and maintain them even when it's challenging

- Reaffirm my value based on who I truly am, not on achievements

I commit to dedicating 15 minutes each day to this work. I understand that growth, like tending a garden, requires patience, consistency, and daily care.

I'm doing this because:

....

....

....

(Write 1-3 deep, honest reasons why you want to free yourself from others' judgments)

I know there will be days when I want to quit. On those days, I will: - Remind myself that discomfort is a sign of growth - Focus only on that day's exercise, not worrying about tomorrow - Remember that small steps matter on the larger journey

I will track my progress by:

1. Noting moments when I choose not to take judgments personally

2. Recognizing when I dedicate energy to building rather than reacting

3. Celebrating small victories along the way

Today, I choose to begin a 60-day journey to become the most authentic and powerful version of myself.

Date: _______ Signature: _______

Contents

YOUR GIFT FOR THE JOURNEY **02**
INTRODUCTION **04**
Your 60-Day Self-Building Commitment **06**
How to Use This Workbook **12**

STAGE 01: LET THEM TALK

PHASE 01: IDENTIFYING PROJECTIONS **20**
Day 1: Detecting Energy Leaks 20
Day 2: The Projection Mirror 22
Day 3: Energy Leak Map 24

PHASE 02: RESET TECHNIQUES **26**
Day 4: Identifying Patterns 26
Day 5: Opinion Sorting 28
Day 6: Reality Filter 30
Day 7: Breaking Loops 32

PHASE 03: RECLAIMED ENERGY **34**
Day 8: Energy Reinvestment 34
Day 9: Let Them Exhaust 36
Day 10: Energy Reclaimed 38
Day 11: Valuable Opinions 40
Day 12: Protection Shield 42

PHASE 04: STRENGTHENING BOUNDARIES **44**
Day 13: Clear Boundaries 44
Day 14: Not My Business List 46
Day 15: Checkpoint - Stage 1 Reflection 48

Mini-Milestone 01 .... **50**

STAGE 02: LET ME FOCUS

PHASE 01: IDENTIFYING ENERGY LEAKS 56

Day 16: Mind Distraction Map 56

Day 17: Classifying Disruptions 58

Day 18: Renewal Cycle 60

Day 19: Transition Effect 62

PHASE 02: BUILDING YOUR INNER SANCTUARY 64

Day 20: Designing Sacred Space 64

Day 21: Focus Ritual 66

Day 22: Incremental Focus Technique 68

Day 23: Unlocking Intrinsic Motivation 70

PHASE 03: THE POWER OF SAYING NO 72

Day 24: Time Inventory 72

Day 25: Graceful Rejection 74

Day 26: Digital Boundaries 77

Day 27: Protecting Social Energy 80

PHASE 04: SOLIDIFYING FOCUS HABITS 83

Day 28: Focus Intensity Scale 83

Day 29: Focus Community 86

Day 30: Checkpoint - Reflecting on Stage 2 89

BONUS SECTION: IMPOSTOR SHIELD (ESPECIALLY FOR WOMEN) 91

Mini-Milestone 02 97

STAGE 03: LET ME GROW

PHASE 01: IDENTIFYING LABELS 102

Day 31: Identity Projection Map 102

Day 32: Hidden Labels Journal 104

Day 33: The "Who Says So?" Investigation 106

Day 34: Chosen vs. Assigned Labels 108

PHASE 02: REMOVING FALSE IDENTITIES **110**
Day 35: Label Removal Challenge 110
Day 36: Separating Behavior from Identity 112
Day 37: New Identity Experience 114
Day 38: Farewell Ritual 116

PHASE 03: REDEFINING YOURSELF **118**
Day 39: Core Values Map 118
Day 40: Value-Based Identity Statement 120
Day 41: Creating New History 122
Day 42: New Identity Reflection 124

PHASE 04: ESTABLISHING YOUR NEW IDENTITY **126**
Day 43: Building a Self-Validation System 126
Day 44: Embodied Identity 128
Day 45: Checkpoint - Reflecting on Stage 3 130

BONUS SECTION: BODY SOVEREIGNTY & SELF-WORTH (ESPECIALLY FOR WOMEN) **133**

Mini-Milestone 03 .... **138**

STAGE 04: LET ME BUILD

PHASE 01: UNINFLUENCED VISION **144**
Day 46: Abandoned Dreams Survey 144
Day 47: Breaking Success Templates 148
Day 48: Exploring Hidden Success 150
Day 49: Authentic Vision Board 153

PHASE 02: BUILDING AUTONOMOUS SYSTEMS **155**
Day 50: Values Compass 155
Day 51: Pressure Journal 160
Day 52: Value-Based Decision Matrix 162
Day 53: Inner Sovereignty System 165

PHASE 03: SKILLS FOR FACING CHALLENGES **167**
Day 54: Trigger Map 167
Day 55: Resilience Response Scripts 170
Day 56: Inner Critic Dialogue 174
Day 57: Discomfort Tolerance Practice 177
PHASE 04: AUTHENTIC LIVING SYSTEMS **180**
Day 58: Reality Check System 180
Day 59: Journey Integration Overview 184
Day 60: Authentic Living Blueprint 186
BONUS SECTION: LIFE HARMONY NAVIGATOR (FOR BUSY WOMEN) **192**
Final Milestone **198**
ONE LAST THING BEFORE YOU GO **200**

How to Use This Workbook

This workbook is designed with the awareness that your life is already busy enough. In a world of hustle culture and toxic productivity, you don't need another lengthy to-do list. You need a system that's simple, powerful, and effective.

- **60 days isn't a long time, but it's enough to create profound change.** Research on habit formation shows that while it takes 66 days for a new habit to become automatic, significant changes begin to appear after 3-4 weeks. We've designed this 60-day journey based on the science of change and habit psychology.
- **Each day requires only 15 minutes of your commitment.** That's shorter than a yoga session, a podcast episode, or the time you spend scrolling through TikTok. Quality matters more than quantity.
- **Each week includes one "deep reflection" day (30 minutes).** This is your opportunity to review your progress, adjust your course, and strengthen your commitment – like a brief personal coaching session with yourself.
- **Flexibility is key.** Fit this workbook into a schedule that works for YOU. Maybe it's morning with your coffee before checking emails, during lunch break instead of scrolling social media, or in the evening before bed. What matters is consistency.

Daily Structure

Each day of this 60-day journey is structured concisely, with power coming from simplicity:

1. Quick Trigger (2 minutes): A brief question or situation that activates your awareness about a specific aspect of how others' opinions affect you. This is your daily "aha" moment that helps you recognize your blind spots.

2. Power Question (3 minutes): A profound, transformative question that unlocks new thinking. Not an ordinary question, but one designed to break old thought patterns and create new neural pathways.

3. **Micro Action (7-10 minutes):** A small action with big impact. Like a rep at your mental gym – not too strenuous but effective when done consistently.

4. **Power Phrase (30 seconds):** A brief, memorable affirmation you can carry throughout your day. Like a personal theme song for the day.

Over 60 days, you'll progress through 4 transformational stages:

- **STAGE 1 (Days 1-15): LET THEM TALK** – Liberation from criticism
- **STAGE 2 (Days 16-30): LET ME FOCUS** – Creating absolute focus space
- **STAGE 3 (Days 31-45): LET ME GROW** – Redefining your authentic self
- **STAGE 4 (Days 46-60): LET ME BUILD** – Creating your own reality

Each stage builds upon the previous one, creating a natural and sustainable transformation process.

Our Promise to You

This isn't your typical self-help book. This isn't another collection of *"productivity hacks"* or *"work smarter, not harder"* tips you've read in countless Medium articles. This is a systematic transformation journey based on neuroscience, positive psychology, and ancient wisdom.

We don't promise overnight changes. But we do commit that if you dedicate 15 minutes each day for the next 60 days, you will:

- Free up hours of mental energy each week from worrying about others' opinions
- Develop immunity to external judgments, from social media to family gatherings
- Build a solid internal system to guide your life according to your values
- Create high-focus spaces to accomplish what truly matters
- Redefine yourself based on core values rather than social pressure

Remember: *"You don't need their approval. You just need to keep building."*

Begin your journey now.

Reminder before starting: Each day in this journey isn't just an exercise, but a step in your transformation process. Treat this book as a faithful companion – non-judgmental, unhurried, always there when you need it. And remember, each time you choose not to take criticism personally, you're watering a seed in your garden.

STAGE 01

LET THEM TALK

Stop worrying what others think, start living your life

01 02 03 04 05 06 07 08 09 10 11 12 13 14 15 16 17 18 19 20
21 22 23 24 25 26 27 28 29 30 31 32 33 34 35 36 37 38 39 40
41 42 43 44 45 46 47 48 49 50 51 52 53 54 55 56 57 58 59 60

Hey, can we get real for a minute?

Does that *"seen"* message with no reply from a friend make you overthink all day? Does a small comment on your Instagram post tank your mood? Or that look from your boss in a meeting that leaves you wondering, *"Did I do something wrong?"*

I get it. I've BEEN there. And trust me—you're not alone.

Try a quick experiment: Check your phone. What did you just do? Did you refresh to see if anyone liked your latest status? Or check if your colleague responded to that important email yet? These days, we've turned seeking feedback from others into a reflex—like we need that dopamine hit of approval.

When was the last time you actually did something WITHOUT caring what others would think? Like, genuinely not caring? Hard to answer, isn't it?

That's exactly why we're starting with *"Let Them Talk."*

The truly wise have understood this for ages. Epictetus (and don't worry, I won't throw too many ancient names at you)—a guy who went from slave to philosopher—basically said: It's not what happens to you that hurts, it's how you react to it.

In other words? That comment on Facebook doesn't ruin your day. How you read and respond to it ruins your day.

In this age of Instagram-perfect, TikTok-viral, and LinkedIn-humble-bragging, we've become approval addicts. We take 50 photos to post one. We draft emails five times before hitting send. We even choose restaurants based on how "Instagrammable" they are. This isn't natural. It's a new kind of addiction we were never equipped to handle.

But imagine for a minute—you wake up tomorrow and suddenly DON'T CARE what others think. Not in a way that hurts people. But in the truly free way—the kind where you can:

- Post a thought on social media without checking your phone 20 times in the next hour
- Speak up in meetings without worrying you'll sound "stupid"
- Wear the outfit YOU like, not the one you think others will approve of
- Pursue a passion without fear people will laugh

That's the kind of freedom we're building in the next 15 days.

Here's the truth: When others judge you, they're not really judging YOU. They're judging their version of you in their head—a version filtered through all their own insecurities, fears, and experiences. As Carl Jung (ok, last name I'm throwing at you, I promise) pointed out, we often *"project"* parts of ourselves onto others. In other words, when someone criticizes you for being *"too ambitious,"* they're likely wrestling with their own fears about not being ambitious enough.

Sound familiar? So in this first section, we're going to do something simple but completely game-changing: we're going to stop taking other people's judgments personally.

This isn't high-level theory. This is about reclaiming your life, one day at a time, from the noise and judgments of others.

Ready to give it a shot? Let's begin.

Our Goals for These 15 Days

It's simple. By the end of Stage 1, you'll:

- Instantly recognize when someone is projecting their issues onto you
- Stop automatically absorbing every criticism as if it's the truth about you
- Save HOURS of mental energy each week by no longer overthinking what others might be thinking
- Begin to feel a sense of lightness and freedom in a way you may not have felt since... middle school?

Our Secret Weapon: Projection Shield Protocol™

For the next 15 days, we'll use a tool I call the **Projection Shield Protocol™**. Sounds complex, but it's surprisingly simple.

What's a Projection Shield? Think of it as an umbrella. When someone pours *"judgment rain"* on you, instead of letting it soak you, you simply put up your umbrella. The judgments still fall, but they no longer saturate you.

Let's be real: People will always have opinions. They'll judge your clothes, your job, who you date, how you parent, and even how you take your coffee. You can't stop them. But you can stop those opinions from shaping your life.

The **Projection Shield Protocol™** will teach you:

1. How to INSTANTLY know when someone is projecting their issues onto you
2. How to separate helpful feedback from toxic garbage
3. How to create a "mental shield" to not absorb negative energy
4. How to redirect saved energy into building the life YOU want

Overview of the 4 Phases

Before we begin, let's better understand the *"map"* we'll follow for the next 15 days. Each phase is designed to build on the previous one, like constructing a house - you can't build walls before laying the foundation. Let's look more closely at why we've organized this journey this way:

PHASE 1: IDENTIFYING PROJECTIONS (Days 1-3)

Why start here? You can't fix a problem you can't see. In these first days, we focus on developing *"mental vision"* - the ability to recognize when someone is projecting their issues onto you.

Imagine wearing special glasses that can detect *"projections"*. Whenever someone says something negative about you, the glasses show whether it's really about you or if it's their fear, insecurity, or issue. It's amazing when you start to see how many comments *"about you"* aren't about you at all!

Main goal: Develop the ability to identify projections and understand how they affect you. When you can see it, you're halfway to freeing yourself from it.

PHASE 2: RESET TECHNIQUES (Days 4-7)

Why this phase next? Once you know how to identify projections, the next step is learning how to not automatically react in old ways. This is where we break long-programmed *"default"* reaction patterns.

Think of it like resetting your Wi-Fi router when it's acting up. Years of enduring criticism, social expectations, and need for approval have created default neural connections in your brain. You're practically programmed to react in certain ways when criticized - too defensive, too apologetic, or too quick to change yourself. This phase is about "resetting" those reactions.

Main goal: Develop tools to stop, think, and choose your response rather than automatically reacting in old patterns. This is when you start to feel real power - when you realize you can CHOOSE how to respond to others' opinions.

PHASE 3: RECLAIMED ENERGY (Days 8-12)

Why is this phase important? When you spend less time worrying about others' opinions, you'll notice something magical - you suddenly have more mental energy! This phase focuses on recognizing and reinvesting this new energy source.

Imagine that each time you worry about someone's opinion, you put a small stone in your backpack. Over the years, you've carried hundreds, even thousands of these invisible stones. No wonder you feel tired! As you start removing these stones, you feel lighter, more focused, and more capable of creating meaningful things.

Main goal: Recognize the freed-up energy and learn to consciously redirect it into building efforts rather than worrying about criticism.

PHASE 4: STRENGTHENING BOUNDARIES (Days 13-15)

Why end with this phase? As you begin living less dependent on others' opinions, you'll need clear boundaries to protect your progress. This is about equipping your *"new self"* with tools to maintain long-term.

Think of boundaries as the security system for your newly built house. You've just created a new mental space where others' opinions have less power. Now you need to ensure that space is protected. This doesn't mean becoming rude or stubborn - it means being able to say *"no, that doesn't serve me"* when necessary.

Main goal: Establish clear, practical boundaries to protect your new mental space, ensuring these changes are sustainable long after the 60 days.

PHASE 01 IDENTIFYING PROJECTIONS

Day 1: Detecting Energy Leaks

Quick Trigger: "What comments from others typically make you feel like you've been punched in the gut?"

....

....

....

....

....

Power Question: "When I receive negative feedback, how much of it is really about me, and how much is about the person giving the feedback?"

....

....

....

....

....

....

Micro Action (7-10 minutes): Create *an Energy Audit* - Take a piece of paper or your phone's Notes app. Draw two columns. Label column 1 "Situations where I worry what others think". Label column 2 "Energy drain (1-10)". List 5-7 situations in your current life. For example:

Situations where I worry what others think	Energy drain (1-10)
• Posting a selfie on Instagram	7
• Speaking up in team meetings	8
• Wearing new clothes to the office	6

Pro tip: This chart isn't to judge you! It's just a way to become more conscious of where you're "leaking" energy. You can't fix what you don't see.

"Their reaction says more about them than about me."

Day 2: The Projection Mirror

Quick Trigger: "Whose opinion stressed me out the most today?"

Power Question: "What is it about this person or our relationship that gives them such 'power' over me?"

Micro Action: Create *a Projection Mirror* - Choose someone whose opinion strongly affects you (could be a boss, partner, parent, or social media follower). Write down 3 criticisms they typically offer. For each criticism, complete the sentence: "This might reflect ___ about them." For example:

Criticism: "You're too sensitive" Might reflect: "They're uncomfortable with emotions and find it difficult to handle when others express feelings"

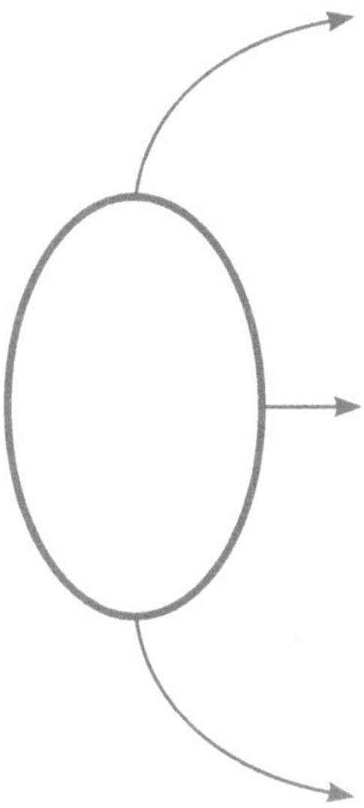

1. ....

This might reflect: ....

....

2. ....

This might reflect: ....

....

3. ....

This might reflect: ....

....

Pro tip: This is NOT about blaming others or avoiding responsibility. It's about recognizing that when someone reacts strongly to you, there's often more going on than meets the eye.

"I see their projection but I don't claim it as mine."

Day 3: Energy Leak Map

Quick Trigger: "How do I change my behavior to avoid being judged?"

Power Question: "If I were completely unconcerned about judgment, what version of myself would show up?"

Micro Action: Draw *an Energy Leak Map* - Draw a circle in the middle of the page with your name (or use a mind-mapping app on your phone). Around it, draw 3-5 smaller circles with the names of people/groups/situations that make you worry about judgment. Draw arrows from your circle to each of these circles, with the thickness of the arrow representing how much energy is being leaked. Mark the 3 thickest arrows - these are where you're losing the most energy.

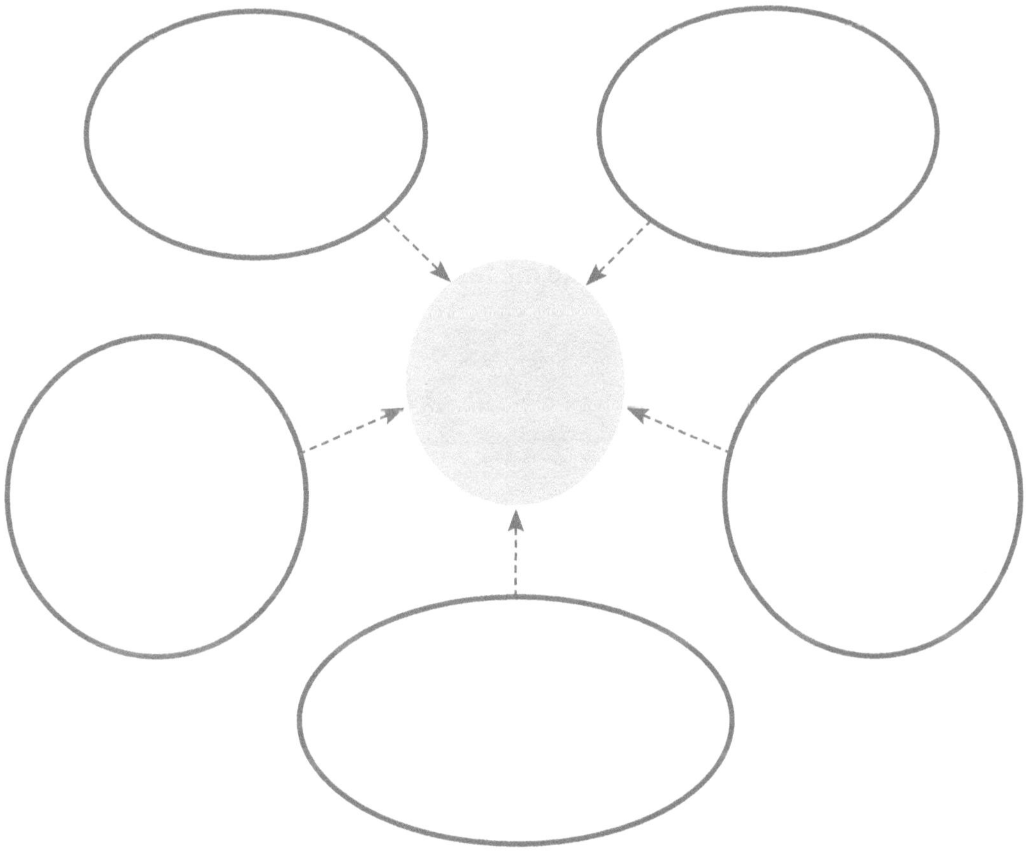

Pro tip: This is where many people get shocked - they don't realize how much energy they're giving to people who aren't even important in their lives! People you only see once a year? Strangers on Instagram? It's crazy to think how much power we give them!

"I see where my energy is leaking and I'm starting to seal the holes."

PHASE 02

RESET TECHNIQUES

Day 4: Identifying Patterns

Quick Trigger: "What situations make me feel like I need to prove myself the most?"

Power Question: "What am I trying to prove, and really to whom?"

Micro Action: Create a Validation Pattern Tracker - Write down 3 recent instances where you felt the need to prove yourself. For each instance, complete these sentences:

- "I felt I needed to prove ___."
- "This feeling reminds me of ___ from my past."
- "If I didn't need to prove anything, I might have ___."

For example:

- "I felt I needed to prove that I deserved the promotion."
- "This feeling reminds me of when my high school teacher said I wasn't smart enough."
- "If I didn't need to prove anything, I might have felt more comfortable proposing new ideas in meetings."

1. ....

....

....

....

....

2. ....

....

....

....

....

3. ....

....

....

....

....

Pro tip: You'll often find that current needs to prove yourself connect to a past wound. When you recognize this, it becomes easier to let go.

"I don't need to prove my worth."

Day 5: Opinion Sorting

Quick Trigger: "Whose opinions truly matter to me and why?"

Power Question: "How can I distinguish between helpful feedback and negative projection?"

Micro Action: Create *an Opinion Sorter* - Draw 3 concentric circles. Label the innermost "Opinions I always need to listen to," the middle one "Opinions worth considering case by case," and the outermost "Regular noise." Fill in names for each circle.

The inner circle should be EXTREMELY selective - people who meet ALL these criteria:

- They truly understand you and your goals
- They want what's best for you
- They have experience in the area they're advising on
- They deliver feedback respectfully

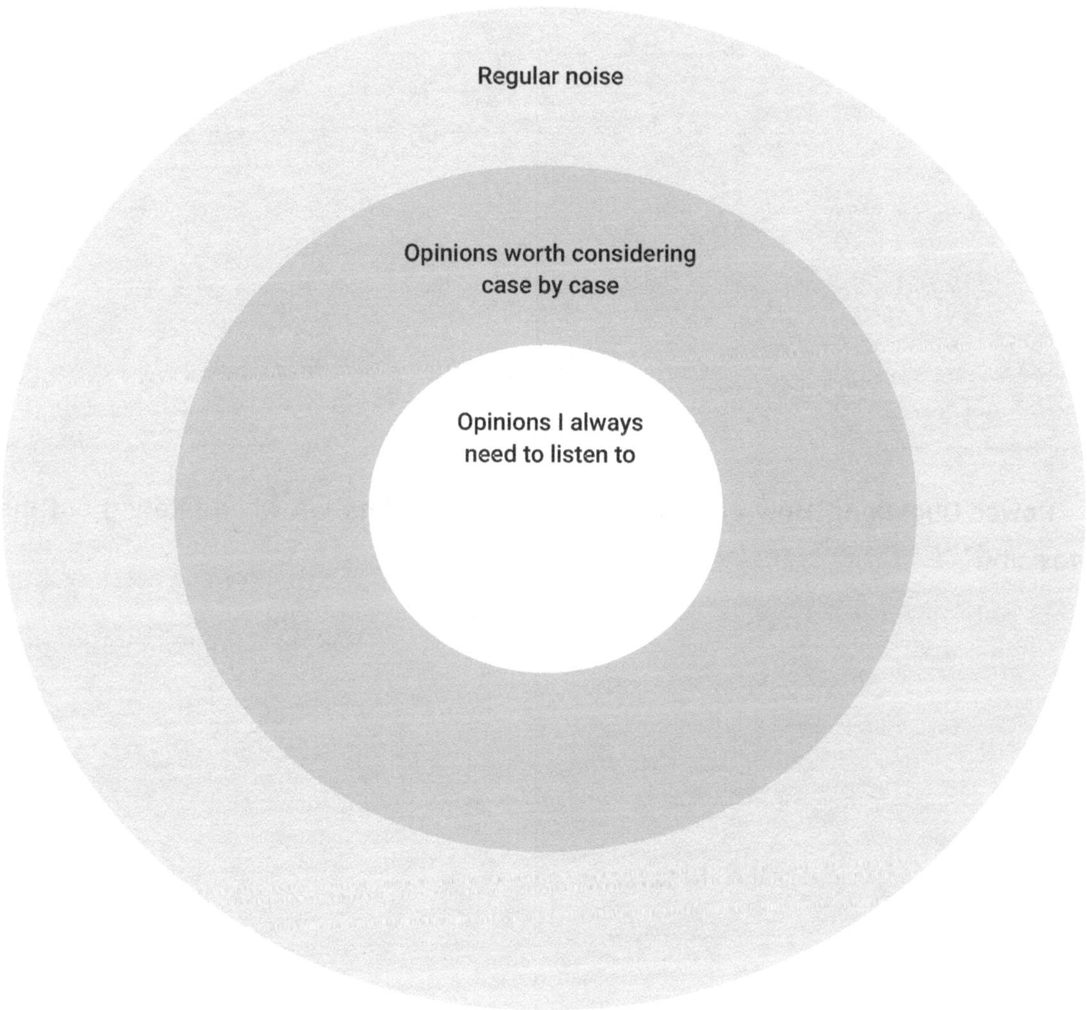

Pro tip: Most people realize their innermost circle has only 3-5 people. That's good! Not everyone deserves an important voice in your life.

"I am selective about the opinions I let in."

Day 6: Reality Filter

Quick Trigger: "When criticized, how do I process it?"

Power Question: "How can I keep the useful information while filtering out the toxicity?"

Micro Action: Create *a Reality Check Filter* - Write down 3 short questions to ask yourself when receiving uncomfortable feedback. For example:

- "Is this really true about me, or is it projection from someone else?"
- "Even if partly true, do I need to react to this right now?"
- "What response would best serve my growth?"

Write these questions on a small card or save them in your phone for easy access when needed.

Pro tip: Create a shortened version of this filter on your phone. When you get a message or email that makes you feel hurt, pause and run it through your filter before responding.

"I have a reality filter to see through projections."

Day 7: Breaking Loops

Quick Trigger: "After being criticized, what thought loops does my mind usually fall into?"

....

....

....

....

....

....

Power Question: "How can I interrupt these negative thought loops?"

....

....

....

....

....

....

Micro Action: Create *a Pattern Interrupt System* - Identify 3 common thought loops you experience when criticized. For example:

- "I'm not good enough" ➔ "I should try harder" ➔ "I'm still not good enough" ➔ ...
- "They think I'm stupid" ➔ "I shouldn't speak up anymore" ➔ "Now they think I have nothing to contribute" ➔ ...

For each loop, write down an immediate pattern-breaking action:

- 3 deep breaths + hand on chest
- Change environment (get water, go outside for 2 minutes)
- Physical movement for 30 seconds (jumping jacks, body twist)

Pro tip: Practice these interruption tools BEFORE you need them. Like muscles, they work better when regularly exercised.

"I have the power to break negative loops anytime."

PHASE 03 RECLAIMED ENERGY

Day 8: Energy Reinvestment

Quick Trigger: "What could I do if I weren't worried about what others think?"

Power Question: "Where can I redirect this energy into something meaningful?"

Micro Action: Create an Energy Redirection Map - Write down 3 activities you genuinely enjoy but often self-censor because of concerns about others' opinions. For each activity, write:

- "What I really want is ___." (e.g., learn to dance, post TikTok cooking videos, start a podcast)
- "What's stopping me is ___." (e.g., fear of looking silly, worry others will criticize)
- "The first small step I could take is ___." (e.g., sign up for a private class, film a video just for close friends)

1. ....

What I really want is ....

What's stopping me is ....

....

The first small step I could take is ....

....

2. ....

What I really want is ....

What's stopping me is ....

....

The first small step I could take is ....

....

3. ....

What I really want is ....

What's stopping me is ....

....

The first small step I could take is ....

....

Pro tip: Actually DO one of those "first small steps" this week. Action, even small, is far more powerful than just thinking about it.

"I choose to invest my energy in what nourishes me."

Day 9: Let Them Exhaust

Quick Trigger: "How much time do I spend imagining conversations with others in my head?"

Power Question: "What if I let others exhaust themselves with what they think about me, while I keep building?"

Micro Action: Practice *Let Them Exhaust* - Choose a recent situation where you were criticized. Write a short paragraph: "They're busy thinking ___ about me. Meanwhile, I'm busy ___."

For example: "They're busy thinking I'm too ambitious for proposing a new project. Meanwhile, I'm busy developing my leadership skills and building my portfolio."

Repeat with 2-3 other situations.

1...

....

....

....

2...

....

....

....

3...

....

....

....

Pro tip: This is one of the most powerful exercises! When you realize that worrying about others' opinions is a FULL-TIME JOB for your MIND, you'll see more clearly than ever why you need to let it go.

"They can exhaust themselves with judgment,
I choose to thrive with creation."

Day 10: Energy Reclaimed

Quick Trigger: "What signs show I'm reclaiming energy from worrying about others' opinions?"

Power Question: "How can I track and celebrate my progress?"

Micro Action: Start *an Energy Reclamation Journal* - Create a small journal on your phone or notebook. Each evening, write down one moment from the day when you chose not to worry about others' opinions, and instead did what you truly wanted. Record:

- "I chose ___ instead of worrying about ___."
- "The energy I reclaimed felt like ___."

For example:

- "I chose to wear my vibrant patterned shirt instead of worrying that coworkers would think it was too loud."
- "The energy I reclaimed felt like a fresh breeze after a stuffy day."

1...

....

....

2...

....

....

3...

....

....

Pro tip: Keep this journal going after the 60 days - it's a great way to track your long-term progress!

"Every moment I don't react is energy I reclaim."

Day 11: Valuable Opinions

Quick Trigger: "Whose opinions do I value and why?"

Power Question: "How do I identify opinions truly worth listening to?"

Micro Action: Create *an Opinion Value Scale* - Draw a horizontal line, with "Noise" at one end and "True Value" at the other. List 5-7 people in your life and place them on this scale. For each person, write down why they're positioned where they are.

Then, mark which opinions you'll consider more and less from now on. Be specific:

- "I'll take ___ opinions about ___ less seriously"
- "I'll value ___ opinions about ___ more"

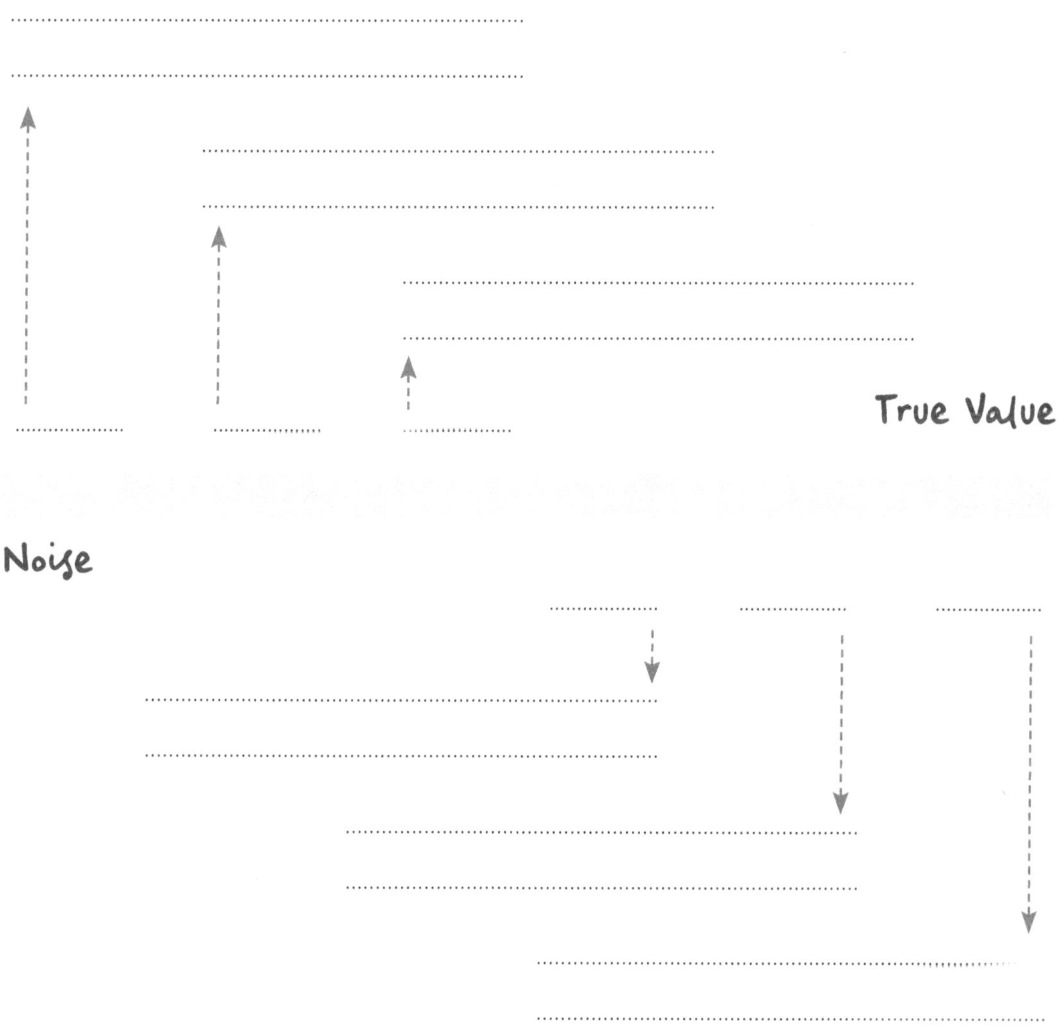

Pro tip: This isn't about judging people's worth. It's about recognizing that not everyone has the capacity or perspective to give good advice on EVERY aspect of your life.

"Not all opinions are created equal."

Day 12: Protection Shield

Quick Trigger: "What reactions from others trigger me the most?"

Power Question: "How can I protect my spirit from negative projections?"

Micro Action: Create *a Projection Protection Protocol* - Write down 3 protection measures when facing projection from others:

1. Immediate reaction: "When feeling attacked, I'll first ___" (e.g., take a deep breath, pause for 5 seconds, place hand on chest)

2. Neutral response: "A neutral statement I can use is ___" (e.g., "I understand that's your perspective," "I'll consider that")

3. Exit technique: "If a situation becomes too negative, I'll ___" (e.g., "Thank you for your perspective, I need time to think about this")

1...

....

....

2...

....

....

3...

....

....

Pro tip: Practice these statements BEFORE you actually need them. When you're in a stressful situation, you'll default to what you've pre-programmed.

"I have a mental protection system against negative projections."

PHASE 04

STRENGTHENING BOUNDARIES

Day 13: Clear Boundaries

Quick Trigger: "What boundaries do I need to establish to protect my energy?"

Power Question: "How can I set boundaries without feeling guilty?"

Micro Action: Create *a Boundary Blueprint* - Identify 3 areas in your life that need new boundaries to protect your energy. For example:

- Work (after-hours emails, weekend messages)
- Social media (usage time, type of content you consume)
- Specific relationships (people who criticize, energy vampires)

For each area, write down:

1. The boundary to establish: "I will ___"
2. Why this boundary matters: "This matters because ___"
3. How you'll communicate it: "I'll say ___"

1. ....

I will ....

This matters because ....

....

I'll say ....

....

2. ....

I will ....

This matters because ....

....

I'll say ....

....

3. ....

I will ....

This matters because ....

....

I'll say ....

....

Pro tip: If you feel guilty setting boundaries, remember: boundaries aren't walls, they're gates. They're not to isolate you, but to protect what's precious - your energy and mental health.

"My boundaries aren't to hurt - they're to heal."

Day 14: Not My Business List

Quick Trigger: "What responsibilities am I carrying that aren't mine?"

Power Question: "What is truly my business, and what isn't?"

Micro Action: Create *a Not My Business List* - Draw two columns. Label the left "Not my business" and the right "Actually my business."

In the left column, list all the things you can't control and aren't your responsibility. In the right column, list what actually is your responsibility. For example:

Not my business	Actually my business
• Others' opinions of me	• How I respond to criticism
• How others respond to my efforts	• The boundaries I set
• Whether people "like" me	• The values I prioritize
• Guessing what others are thinking	• How I invest my time and energy

Not my business	Actually my business

Pro tip: Keep this list handy! It's one of the most powerful tools to quickly get you back in your "lane" when you start worrying about things outside your control.

"I don't carry what isn't mine."

Day 15: Checkpoint - Stage 1 Reflection

Quick Trigger: "What has changed in the past 15 days about how I view others' opinions?"

Power Question: "What have I learned about myself and how others project onto me?"

Micro Action:

- Spend 15 minutes deeply reflecting on your entire Stage 1 journey
- Review all your completed notes and exercises
- Write down the 3-5 most important discoveries you've made

....

....

....

....

....

....

- Identify 2-3 new habits you want to maintain from this phase

....

....

....

....

....

....

Pro tip: Celebrate your progress! Research shows the brain remembers positive celebration moments, making new habits more likely to stick.

"I'm becoming more immune to others' opinions and freer to build every day."

Mini-Milestone 01

YASSS! You did it! First 15 days, done √

I want you to pause for a moment and REALLY RECOGNIZE what you've just accomplished:

- You've learned to identify when others' reactions are about them, not you
- You've developed a system to categorize and filter others' opinions
- You've begun building mental shields against negative projections
- You've identified necessary boundaries to protect your energy

To acknowledge this progress, complete the following sentence and record it in your journal:

"I've freed up ___ hours/week from worrying about others' opinions and invested in ________________________________ instead."

For example: "I've freed up 8 hours/week from worrying about others' opinions and invested in my new podcast instead."

Don't worry - this is just the beginning. In the next stage, we'll learn not only to free energy from others' opinions but to create absolute focus space to build what matters most to you.

Remember: "They can exhaust themselves with judgment. I'll be busy building."

> **Share your journey:** If you feel comfortable, share one important lesson you've realized over the past 15 days on social media with hashtag #LetThemTalkLetMeBuild. Sometimes, sharing your journey can help others find strength for their own.

STAGE 02

LET ME FOCUS

Building an Impenetrable Focus Space

01 02 03 04 05 06 07 08 09 10 11 12 13 14 15 16 17 18 19 20
21 22 23 24 25 26 27 28 29 30 31 32 33 34 35 36 37 38 39 40
41 42 43 44 45 46 47 48 49 50 51 52 53 54 55 56 57 58 59 60

Dear friend,

Wow, you've completed Stage 1! I'm truly proud of you. You've begun building immunity to others' opinions - but this is just the first step.

Now for the important question: After freeing yourself from the *"noise"* of others, what will you do with this new space?

Because here's the truth: Simply stopping worrying about others' opinions is NOT the final destination. That's just clearing the space. The next step? Building something meaningful in that space.

Imagine your mind as a garden. In Stage 1, you pulled out the weeds (worrying about others' opinions). In Stage 2, we'll start planting seeds (your ideas, projects, and dreams).

But there's a problem: The modern world is designed to STEAL your focus.

Phone notifications? Ping. New email? Ping. Friends texting? Ping. News? Ping. Social media? PING PING PING.

Each of these *"pings"* isn't just a sound - it's a mental anchor pulling your mind out of your inner space. It pulls you back into a reactive state, worrying about others' opinions, and away from what truly matters to you.

In a world where trillion-dollar tech companies compete for every second of your attention, the ability to focus deeply is the real SUPERPOWER.

That's exactly what we'll build in this Stage 2.

Our secret weapon: Inner Sanctuary Protocol™

The **Inner Sanctuary Protocol™** is a method I developed after working with hundreds of clients overwhelmed by the constant *"noise"* of modern life. It's designed to help you:

1. Recognize when you're getting caught up in *"noise"* that isn't yours
2. Create an inner space that external noise cannot penetrate
3. Develop the ability to gracefully say *"no"* to what interrupts your inner space
4. Maintain a state of deep focus to build what truly matters

How is this different from *"Let Them Talk"* in Stage 1? Stage 1 was about freeing you from the need for approval. Stage 2 is about using that freedom to build something meaningful - by protecting your time and focus as your most precious assets.

Author Cal Newport calls this *"Deep Work"* - the ability to focus without distraction on a difficult task. And he's right - this is the rarest, most valuable skill in the age of information overload.

So enough talking. Let's start building your impenetrable focus space.

Overview of the 4 Phases

Before we begin, let's understand more about the "map" we'll follow over the next 15 days. Each phase is designed to build upon the previous one, similar to building a fortress - you can't construct walls and watchtowers before understanding the terrain. Let's examine in more detail why we've arranged this journey in this way:

PHASE 1: IDENTIFYING ENERGY LEAKS (Days 16-19)

Why start here? You cannot protect what you don't realize is being stolen. In the first few days, we focus on developing a "distraction radar" - the ability to recognize what's stealing your focus and how much time/energy these thieves consume.

Imagine your mind as a bucket full of precious water (mental energy), but this bucket is leaking through many small holes. Before you can use the water effectively, you need to know exactly where the leaks are and how big they are. Consciously patching each leak will help you retain more energy for things that truly matter.

Main objective: Precisely identify what's stealing your focus, what times of day you're most vulnerable, and understand the extent of their impact on your ability to concentrate.

PHASE 2: BUILDING YOUR INNER SANCTUARY (Days 20-23)

Why this phase next? After recognizing what's stealing your focus, you need a safe space where your mind can work without intrusion. This is when we build your mental "sanctuary" - where you can focus deeply without interruption.

Imagine your mind as a vast forest. Most people leave their entire forest open for anyone to pass through, with all kinds of noise, invasions, and interruptions. What we're doing here is creating a sacred protected area within that forest - a space where you control who and what is allowed in. Not the entire forest is protected - just a special space dedicated to creativity and deep focus.

Main objective: Design and build a physical and mental space where you can practice deep focus without interruption, along with rituals and habits to activate this focus state at will.

PHASE 3: THE POWER OF SAYING NO (Days 24-27)

Why is this phase important? Once you've built your focus space, you need to learn how to protect it - and that requires the ability to gracefully decline requests that don't align with your priorities.

Think of it as placing a guard at the entrance to your mental sanctuary. This guard isn't rude or aggressive - they're polite, respectful, but firm. They know who and what should be allowed in, and have the ability to decline everything else without causing unnecessary conflict. This is a skill most of us weren't taught - but it's one of the most important skills for modern life.

Main objective: Develop the ability to identify which demands on your time/energy are worthwhile and which aren't, along with specific scripts and strategies to gracefully decline without damaging relationships.

PHASE 4: SOLIDIFYING FOCUS HABITS (Days 28-30)

Why end with this phase? Building a focus space is only valuable if you actually use it consistently. This final phase is about turning the tools and strategies you've learned into automatic habits for long-term maintenance.

Imagine you've just learned a new sport. You've learned the basic techniques, but only through regular practice do these movements become second nature. Similarly, the ability to focus deeply is a skill that needs to be trained to the point of automation. In this phase, we build systems and processes to ensure these changes become a natural part of how you operate.

Main objective: Create systems, habits, and support networks to ensure that deep focus ability becomes a sustainable part of your daily life, not just during these 15 days but long after the program ends.

When you complete all four phases, you won't just have built an inner space immune to distraction - you'll have developed one of the rarest and most valuable superpowers in the information age: the ability to focus intentionally and deeply. This isn't just a skill for working more effectively - it's the key to living a meaningful and purposeful life in a world that constantly demands our attention.

PHASE 01

IDENTIFYING ENERGY LEAKS

Day 16: Mind Distraction Map

Quick Trigger: "What things most often distract me and break my focus?"

Power Question: "What would happen if I protected my focus like I protect money in my bank account?"

Micro Action: Create *a Distraction Map* - Track every time you get distracted during 4 consecutive hours of work (or study). Use your phone or a small piece of paper to simply record:

- Type of interruption (message, email, thinking about something else, etc.)
- Time it takes to get back to focus
- Feeling after being interrupted (annoyed, curious, relieved?)

At the end of 4 hours, count the total number of interruptions and estimate the total time lost. You'll be surprised by this number.

Type of interruption	Time it takes to get back to focus	Feeling after being interrupted

Pro tip: Don't try to avoid all distractions during this exercise! The purpose is to observe and record, not to fight them. The first step in changing any habit is clear awareness of it.

"I recognize what's stealing my focus."

Day 17: Classifying Disruptions

Quick Trigger: "What 'noise' am I getting caught up in that isn't mine?"

....

....

....

....

....

....

....

....

Power Question: "Where is the boundary between caring attention and having my energy drained?"

....

....

....

....

....

....

....

....

Micro Action: Create *an "Energy Leak Audit"* - Draw three columns on a piece of paper or electronic document:

- "External disruptions" (messages, emails, calls, social media)
- "Internal disruptions" (worries, thinking about past/future, self-criticism)
- "Level of necessity" (scale 1-10: 1 = completely unnecessary, 10 = truly necessary)

List the 5 biggest sources of mental energy drain in each column. For example:

- Checking email every 15 minutes (2/10)
- Worrying about next week's meeting (3/10)
- Group messages unrelated to work (1/10)

External disruptions	Internal disruptions	Level of necessity

Pro tip: Anything rated below 5/10 should be considered for immediate elimination or reduction! Be honest - how many things that occupy your mental space are truly IMPORTANT?

"I can distinguish between noise and valuable information."

Day 18: Renewal Cycle

Quick Trigger: "When do I feel most exhausted during the day?"

Power Question: "How can I protect and renew my mental energy?"

Micro Action: Create *an Energy Renewal Cycle* - Track your mental energy level throughout a day, rating from 1-10 every 2 hours. Identify:

- "Golden hours" - when you feel most alert and focused
- "Dip times" - when you feel tired or easily distracted
- "Energy-draining activities" - things that make your energy level drop quickly
- "Energy-charging activities" - things that make you feel refreshed and more focused

Design a work/study schedule that utilizes your "golden hours" for tasks requiring the highest focus, and place "energy-charging activities" during your "dip times."

Timeline	Golden hours	Dip times	Energy-draining activities	Energy-charging activities
	▢	▢	▢	▢
	▢	▢	▢	▢
	▢	▢	▢	▢
	▢	▢	▢	▢
	▢	▢	▢	▢
	▢	▢	▢	▢
	▢	▢	▢	▢
	▢	▢	▢	▢
	▢	▢	▢	▢
	▢	▢	▢	▢
	▢	▢	▢	▢

Pro tip: Most people have two "golden hours" each day - typically early morning and late afternoon. Protect these time slots from meetings and simple tasks. Reserve them for your most important work.

"I respect and leverage the natural rhythm of my energy."

Day 19: Transition Effect

Quick Trigger: "Each time I'm interrupted, how long does it take me to get back to a state of focus?"

Power Question: "How can I minimize the 'switching cost' when I must transition between tasks?"

Micro Action: Practice *Task Transition Training* - Today, experiment with working in protected time blocks:

1. Choose an important task
2. Set a timer for 25 minutes
3. During those 25 minutes:
    - Turn off all notifications
    - Put your phone in airplane mode or in another room
    - Close all unrelated browser tabs
    - Let people around you know not to disturb you
4. Work on only one task for the entire 25 minutes
5. Record:
    - How many times you felt the urge to switch to something else

....

....

    - Your progress level compared to your "normal" way of working

....

....

    - How you feel after completing 25 minutes of focus

....

....

Pro tip: Research shows that each time you're interrupted, you can lose up to 23 minutes to get back to a complete state of focus! This is not a small issue - that's why protecting your focus space is so important.

"Every switch has a cost. I protect my flow of focus."

PHASE 02

BUILDING YOUR INNER SANCTUARY

Day 20: Designing Sacred Space

Quick Trigger: "How is my inner space being invaded?"

Power Question: "How can I create a peaceful inner space amid external noise?"

Micro Action: Design your *"Focus Sanctuary"* - Create a physical and mental space dedicated to focus:

1. Physical space:
   - Choose a specific area (desk corner, room, quiet café)
   - Remove distracting elements (phone, notifications)
   - Add focus-encouraging elements (plants, good lighting, instrumental music if helpful)
2. Mental space:
   - Create a starting ritual (3 deep breaths, affirmation, sip of tea/coffee)
   - Commit to 30 minutes of complete focus on "what I'm building"
   - Create an ending ritual (note progress, gentle stretching, celebrate achievements)

....

....

....

....

....

....

Pro tip: The brain responds powerfully to rituals. When you perform the same sequence of actions before beginning focused work, your brain will start associating that sequence with a state of focus. After a few weeks, just starting the ritual will put you in a focused state.

"I create sacred space for my focus."

Day 21: Focus Ritual

Quick Trigger: "What gets me into a state of focus fastest?"

Power Question: "How can I 'hack' my brain to enter a state of focus at will?"

Micro Action: Develop *a Focus Trigger Routine* - Design a specific 3-step sequence to activate your focus state:

1. Prepare the environment:
   - Clean your workspace
   - Prepare all necessary materials/tools
   - Remove distracting elements
2. Prepare physically:
   - Drink a glass of water
   - Take 5 deep breaths
   - Perform a specific action (like putting on headphones, wearing reading glasses)
3. Prepare mentally:
   - Clearly identify the goal for the work session
   - Write down 1-3 specific outcomes you want to achieve
   - Say your focus affirmation out loud

Practice this entire routine before starting 3 focused work sessions tomorrow.

....

....

....

....

....

....

....

Pro tip: Consistency is the key here. It doesn't matter what your routine is, as long as you perform similar steps each time. This creates a "Pavlovian effect" - your brain begins to associate the routine with a state of deep focus.

"I can activate a state of focus at will."

Day 22: Incremental Focus Technique

Quick Trigger: "How long can I focus continuously before feeling tired?"

Power Question: "How can I expand my capacity to focus without burning out?"

Micro Action: Practice *Focus Expansion Technique* - Build your focus capacity like you would train a muscle:

1. Start with 3 focus sessions, each:
   - 25 minutes of deep focus
   - 5 minutes of rest (stand up, stretch, drink water)
2. In each session, record:
   - When your mind first begins to wander
   - What pulls your attention away
   - How quickly you bring your focus back
3. Each day, try increasing the focus time by 1-2 minutes, or add one more focus session. The goal is to gradually build up to 4-5 sessions per day, each 25-45 minutes.

....

....

....

....

....

....

....

....

....

Pro tip: Don't jump from 25 minutes to 2 hours! Focus ability is like a muscle - it develops gradually over time with consistent practice. Better to have 3 high-quality 25-minute focus sessions than 1 two-hour session with most of the time distracted.

"I build my focus strength daily, one small step at a time."

Day 23: Unlocking Intrinsic Motivation

Quick Trigger: "What gets me so excited that I lose track of time?"

Power Question: "How can I reconnect with the intrinsic motivation behind the work I'm doing?"

Micro Action: Create *an Intrinsic Motivation Map* - Reconnect with the deeper reason behind what you're building:

1. Choose a project or goal you're pursuing
2. Complete the following sentences (write them down, don't just think about them):
   - "I'm building this because ___."
   - "When I complete it, I will feel ___."
   - "This matters to me because ___."
   - "If I don't do this, I will regret ___."
   - "The most exciting part of this project is ___."
3. Find at least three intrinsic motivating factors (not money or recognition) that make you care about this project.
4. Place this motivation map where you can see it while working.

....

....

....

....

....

....

....

....

....

Pro tip: Extrinsic motivation (money, recognition, rewards) depletes quickly. Intrinsic motivation (passion, curiosity, personal challenge) is an endless source of energy for deep focus. When feeling distracted, look back at this map and remind yourself WHY this matters to YOU.

"I connect with the deep source of motivation within me."

PHASE 03

THE POWER OF SAYING NO

Day 24: Time Inventory

Quick Trigger: "What/who am I allowing to invade my space?"

Power Question: "How can I balance being helpful with protecting my time?"

Micro Action: Conduct *a Time Inventory* - Track all requests for your time over the course of a day:

Create three columns in your notebook:

- "Person/Situation requesting my time"
- "Actual value level (1-10)"
- "My response (agree/decline/delay)"

Record every request for your time in the next 24 hours:

- Direct requests (meetings, calls, conversations)
- Digital requests (emails, messages, notifications)
- Implicit requests (feeling you should check email, social media)

Review at the end of the day - you'll be surprised at how many things are demanding your time and how many times you automatically say "yes".

Person/Situation requesting my time	Actual value level (1–10)	My response	Type of request
Manager asked for urgent report	9	Agree	Direct request
Slack message from colleague	5	Delay	Digital request
Thought about checking Instagram	2	Decline	Implicit request
Friend invited me to lunch	6	Agree	Direct request

Person/Situation requesting my time	Actual value level (1–10)	My response	Type of request

Pro tip: Time, unlike money, cannot be earned back. When you realize that every "yes" to someone else is a "no" to yourself and your projects, you'll begin to consider more carefully what you agree to.

"Time is my most precious asset. I invest it consciously."

Day 25: Graceful Rejection

Quick Trigger: "In what situations do I find it hardest to say no?"

Power Question: "How can I decline gracefully without hurting others?"

Micro Action: Develop *"Graceful No Scripts"* - Write 5 polite rejection scripts for the most common situations you encounter:

1. Identify 5 situations where you typically find it difficult to say no:
   - Request for a meeting when you're focused
   - Social invitation when you need time for a personal project
   - Request to work outside your responsibilities
   - etc.
2. For each situation, write a rejection script with 3 parts:
   - Acknowledgment - "Thank you for thinking of me..."
   - Clear decline - "At present I cannot take on more projects..."
   - Alternative (optional) - "However, I can refer you to..."
3. Practice saying these aloud, so they feel natural.

1. ....

Acknowledgment ....

....

Clear decline ....

....

Alternative (optional) ....

....

2. ....

Acknowledgment ....

....

Clear decline ....

....

Alternative (optional) ....

....

3. ....

Acknowledgment ....

....

Clear decline ....

....

Alternative (optional) ....

....

4. ....

Acknowledgment ....

....

Clear decline ....

....

Alternative (optional) ....

....

5. ....

Acknowledgment ....

....

Clear decline ....

....

Alternative (optional) ....

....

Pro tip: Saying no isn't about saying "I'm too busy" - because that just says the other person isn't important enough. Instead, focus on your current commitments: "To do justice to my current projects, I'm guarding my time quite carefully."

"Declining a request doesn't mean rejecting the person."

Day 26: Digital Boundaries

Quick Trigger: "Which technology causes the most distraction for me?"

Power Question: "How can I control technology instead of being controlled by it?"

Micro Action: Establish ***a Digital Boundary Protocol*** - Create a clear boundary system for technology use:

1. Check your screen time on your phone/computer
2. Identify the 3 apps/websites that consume most of your time
3. Create specific boundaries for each app:
   - Time of day allowed (e.g., only after 6 pm)
   - Maximum duration (e.g., 30 minutes/day)
   - Physical space allowed (e.g., no phone in bedroom)
4. Set up supporting tools:
   - Blocking apps for phone/computer
   - Timers for social media usage
   - Automatic "Do Not Disturb" settings

App / Website	Avg. Daily Screen Time	Time of Day Allowed	Max Duration per Day	Allowed Physical Space	Support Tools Enabled
Instagram	1h 20m	After 7 PM only	30 minutes	Not in bedroom	Screen timer, Focus mode
YouTube	2h	Weekends only	45 minutes	Desk only	App blocker, Do Not Disturb
TikTok	2h 30m	After work (post-6 PM)	20 minutes	Not during meals	Social media limiter

App / Website	Avg. Daily Screen Time	Time of Day Allowed	Max Duration per Day	Allowed Physical Space	Support Tools Enabled

Pro tip: A simple but powerful trick: Place your phone in another room when working. Research shows that just having your phone in sight (even when turned off) reduces cognitive capacity!

"Technology is my tool, not my master."

Day 27: Protecting Social Energy

Quick Trigger: "Who in my life drains my energy the most?"

....

....

....

....

Power Question: "How can I maintain healthy relationships while protecting my inner space?"

....

....

....

....

....

Micro Action: Create *a Social Energy Map* - Map the impact of relationships on your ability to focus:

1. Draw 3 concentric circles:
   - Inner circle: "Energy givers" - people who make you feel energized, supported
   - Middle circle: "Neutral" - neither clearly giving nor draining energy
   - Outer circle: "Energy drainers" - after interacting with them, you feel exhausted
2. Place the names of important people in your life in the appropriate circle
3. For people in the outer circle, write a specific strategy:
   - How to reduce exposure time
   - What boundaries to establish
   - Scripts to end interactions when needed

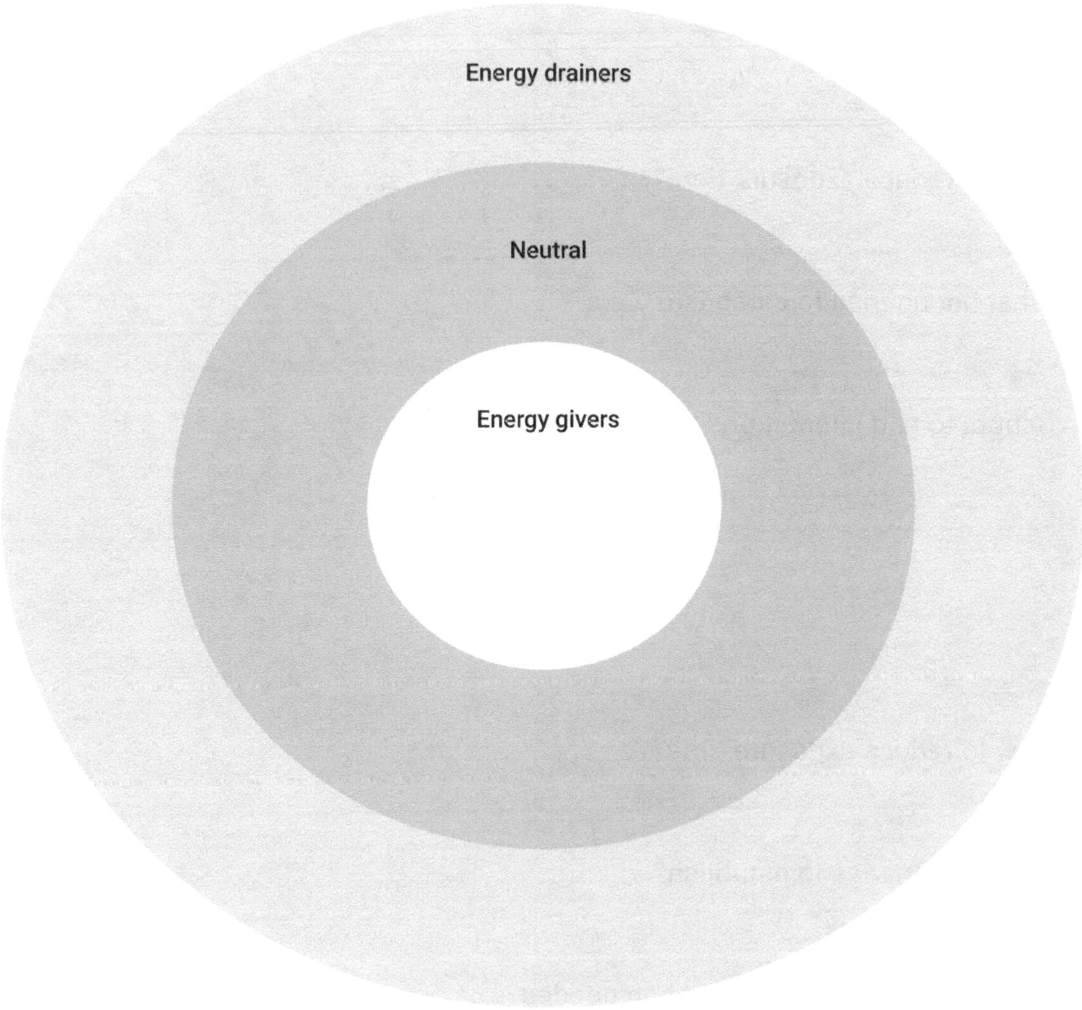

1. ....

How to reduce exposure time? ....

....

What boundaries to establish? ....

....

Scripts to end interactions when needed? ....

....

2. ....

How to reduce exposure time? ....

....

What boundaries to establish? ....

....

Scripts to end interactions when needed? ....

....

3. ....

How to reduce exposure time? ....

....

What boundaries to establish? ....

....

Scripts to end interactions when needed? ....

....

Pro tip: This isn't about completely avoiding energy-draining people - sometimes that's not possible (like family or colleagues). This is about being more conscious in how you interact - perhaps limiting time, meeting them when you have more energy, or preparing mentally before interactions.

"I actively choose how I invest my social energy."

PHASE 04

SOLIDIFYING FOCUS HABITS

Day 28: Focus Intensity Scale

Quick Trigger: "Which work requires the highest level of focus from me?"

Power Question: ""How can I match my focus level to the requirements of each task?"

Micro Action: Create *a "Focus Intensity Scale"* - A scale of focus levels by hour:

1. Create a scale from 1-3:
   - Level 1: Light focus - can handle interruptions (email, routine meetings)
   - Level 2: Medium focus - needs some workspace (analysis, planning)
   - Level 3: Deep focus - no interruptions, all notifications off (creative work, complex problem-solving)
2. Schedule tomorrow, assigning each time block an appropriate focus level
3. Set up appropriate conditions for each level (space, notifications, your availability)
4. Communicate with relevant people about this schedule and when you can/cannot be interrupted

Time Block	Focus Level (1–3)	Task Type / Purpose	Type of request	Required Conditions (space, tools, state)	Notification Settings	Notes for Others
06:00 – 07:00	3	Journaling & daily planning	Direct request	Quiet room, natural light, warm drink, no devices	All notifications off	Do not disturb during this time

Time Block	Focus Level (1–3)	Task Type / Purpose	Type of request	Required Conditions (space, tools, state)	Notification Settings	Notes for Others

Pro tip: Not every task requires deep focus, and that's good! Trying to maintain a high-focus state all day is unrealistic and will lead to burnout. Be strategic about when and how you use your deep focus capacity.

"I match my focus level to the requirements of each task."

Day 29: Focus Community

Quick Trigger: "Who in my life supports and respects my focus space?"

Power Question: "How can I build a support network for my focus goals?"

Micro Action: Build *a Focus Accountability System* - Create an accountability system with those around you:

1. Identify 1-3 people you trust who also want to improve their focus ability
2. Propose a 7-day challenge:
   - Each person commits to 3 deep focus sessions of 25 minutes each day
   - Share specific goals for each session
   - Check in with each other at the end of the day about progress
3. Discuss which strategies worked and didn't work
4. If you can't find partners, create a self-accountability system:
   - Set your timer publicly (with colleagues or family)
   - Share specific goals with someone else before you start
   - Report results to them after completion

7-DAY FOCUS CHALLENGE TRACKER

Day	Session 1 Time	Session 1 Goal	Session 2 Time	Session 2 Goal	Session 3 Time	Session 3 Goal
Mon						
Tue						
Wed						
Thu						
Fri						
Sat						
Sun						

Accountability Partner List

Member	Contact Info	Daily Commitment	Progress Check-In Method

End-of-Day / Weekly Reflection

- What worked well: ....
- What didn't work: ....
- Adjustments for tomorrow/next week: ....

....

If You Don't Have a Partner – Create Self-Accountability

Personal Commitment	Who You ShareIt With	How You'll Track It	How You'll Report Results
3 sessions/ day	Sibling/coworker	Post it on your wall	Send daily summary message

Pro tip: "Peer pressure" can be extremely powerful when used correctly. Knowing that someone else is waiting for your results can be a strong motivator to maintain commitment. Even short check-ins via messages can make a big difference.

"I build a community that supports my focus goals."

Day 30: Checkpoint - Reflecting on Stage 2

Quick Trigger: "What has changed in the past 15 days about my ability to focus?"

Power Question: "What have I learned about protecting my inner space?"

Micro Action:

1. Spend 20 minutes deeply reflecting on the entire Stage 2 journey
2. Reread all completed notes and exercises
3. Write down:
   - 3 most powerful new focus habits you've developed
   - 2 biggest challenges that remain
   - 3 most effective strategies for protecting your time and focus
4. Create a commitment to continue 3 specific habits from this stage

....

....

....

....

....

....

....

....

....

....

....

....

Pro tip: Not every strategy works for everyone. What matters is finding what works for YOU, with your natural rhythm and specific circumstances. Consistently applying your 3 strongest habits is better than trying to implement all 15 habits inconsistently.

"I am building a focus superpower in a distracted world."

BONUS SECTION: IMPOSTOR SHIELD (ESPECIALLY FOR WOMEN)

Exercise 1: Impostor Detector

Quick Trigger: "When do I feel not good enough, not deserving of my current position?"

Power Question: "How can I distinguish between impostor syndrome and realistic assessment of my skills?"

Micro Action: Create *an Impostor Pattern Journal* - Track when impostor syndrome appears:

1. Over the next 3 days, whenever you feel "not good enough" or "just lucky to have this position," record:
   - The situation triggering this feeling
   - Specific thoughts appearing in your mind
   - Physical reactions (racing heart, tension, etc.)
   - Subsequent behavior (avoidance, overworking, etc.)
2. After 3 days, look for patterns:
   - Which situations typically trigger this feeling?
   - Who is usually present when you feel this way?
   - What specific stories repeat in your head?
3. Write down 3 specific warning signs to recognize when you're falling into this pattern.

DAILY TRACKING (DAY 1–3)

Date	Triggering Situation	Thoughts in Your Mind	Physical Reactions (body)	Subsequent Behavior	Notes
	Presenting in front of the boss	I'm not good enough	Racing heartbeat, sweating, stomach pain...	Avoiding, staying silent	wanting to withdraw...

Date	Triggering Situation	Thoughts in Your Mind	Physical Reactions (body)	Subsequent Behavior	Notes

Pattern Review (After 3 Days)

- What situations typically trigger this feeling?

- Who is usually present when you feel this way?

- What specific stories repeat in your head?

Write down 3 specific warning signs to recognize when you're falling into this pattern.

Pro tip: Research shows impostor syndrome affects about 70% of people at some point, but women and people from minority groups often experience it more severely. Recognizing this as a common phenomenon can help you see it as less personal.

"I recognize when impostor syndrome appears and know it's not the truth about me."

Exercise 2: Achievements Reality Check

Quick Trigger: "How do I typically deny or minimize my achievements?"

Power Question: "How can I acknowledge and trust my true capabilities?"

Micro Action: Create *an Evidence Portfolio* - A repository of actual achievements to reference when self-doubt strikes:

1. Create a document or phone note with 3 sections:
   - Past achievements (degrees, successful projects, promotions)
   - Positive feedback (from bosses, colleagues, clients)
   - Challenges overcome (difficult situations you handled successfully)
2. For each item, write:
   - Concrete facts (not feelings or opinions)
   - Skills/qualities you demonstrated
   - Why this matters
3. Update this list regularly and review it whenever impostor syndrome appears.

EVIDENCE PORTFOLIO – REAL ACHIEVEMENTS LOG

Category	Concrete Example (Factual)	Skills / Qualities Demonstrated	Why This Matt
Past Achievement			
Positive Feedback			
Challenge Overcome			

Pro tip: Treat this list as a living document - add to it regularly, even small achievements. Psychological research shows that recording achievements concretely makes them more real in your mind and harder to dismiss when impostor syndrome strikes.

"My achievements are real, not random or lucky."

Mini-Milestone 02

CONGRATULATIONS! You've completed the first 30 days of the journey!

This is when I want you to pause and recognize what you've accomplished:

- You've learned to identify and free yourself from the need for others' approval
- You've built a peaceful inner space amid constant noise
- You've developed the focus superpower in an age of distraction
- You've learned to gracefully decline what doesn't serve your goals

To acknowledge this progress, complete the following sentence and record it in your journal:

"I have created ___ hours of deep focus per week and reduced interruptions from others' opinions/reactions by ___."

Example: "I have created 10 hours of deep focus per week and reduced interruptions from others' opinions/reactions by 70%."

The amazing thing is: these hours of deep focus are worth MANY TIMES MORE than regular working hours. One hour of deep focus can be equivalent to 3-5 hours of constantly distracted work!

In the upcoming Stage 3, we'll learn how to move from protecting your focus space to using that space to build extraordinary things. We'll explore how to harness the Flow state - the ultra-productive psychological state that Olympic athletes and great creators know how to utilize.

Remember: "The age of the focused has returned. In a world of information overload, the ability to focus deeply is the new superpower."

Share your journey: If you feel comfortable, share one of the most effective focus strategies you've learned in the past 15 days on social media with the hashtag #LetThemTalkLetMeBuild. Together, we can create a movement of focus in the age of distraction.

STAGE 03

LET ME GROW

Redefining Your Identity Independent of Judgment

01 02 03 04 05 06 07 08 09 10 11 12 13 14 15 16 17 18 19 20
21 22 23 24 25 26 27 28 29 30 31 32 33 34 35 36 37 38 39 40
41 42 43 44 45 46 47 48 49 50 51 52 53 54 55 56 57 58 59 60

Dear friend,

It's amazing to think about the journey you've been on up to this point. In Stage 1, you learned to free yourself from the need for approval from others. In Stage 2, you built and protected your focus space. Now, we enter the most important journey - returning to yourself.

Because here's the truth: When we spend too much time worrying about what others think, we gradually lose our sense of who we really are. We become a collection of definitions imposed on us by others.

- *"The perfectionist."*
- *"The person who never takes risks."*
- *"The people pleaser." "The overly ambitious one."*
- *"The careful one."*
- *"The undisciplined one."*

None of these labels is you. They're just stories - created by others, then retold by yourself, until you begin to believe they're the truth about who you are.

Over the next 15 days, we'll undertake the most revolutionary work: redefining who you are based on internal values and truths, not external labels.

This isn't about creating a *"better version"* of old definitions. This is about completely breaking the old framework and rebuilding from scratch, on a more solid foundation - one that cannot be shaken by opinions or criticism from others.

Our secret weapon: Authentic Self Reclamation™

Authentic Self Reclamation™ is a method I developed after working with people who had spent most of their lives living according to others' expectations. This is a powerful process that helps you:

1. Identify labels you've unconsciously accepted from others
2. Consciously remove these false identities
3. Redefine yourself based on core values and internal truths
4. Build a self-validation system that doesn't depend on external judgment

How is this different from Stages 1 and 2? Stage 1 helped free you from the need for approval. Stage 2 taught you to protect your focus space. Stage 3 goes even deeper - it doesn't just change how you react to the outside world but changes how you see yourself from within.

Overview of the 4 Phases

Before we begin, let's understand more about the "map" we'll follow over the next 15 days. Each phase is designed to build upon the previous one, similar to restoring an ancient painting - you must carefully remove the layer of dirt before you can see the true colors underneath. Let's examine in more detail why we've arranged this journey in this way:

PHASE 1: IDENTIFYING LABELS (Days 31-34)

Why start here? You cannot change what you're not aware of. In the first few days, we focus on developing "inner vision" - the ability to see the labels, definitions, and stories you've unconsciously accepted from others.

Imagine you're wearing a coat made of many different fabric pieces. Each piece represents a label others have attached to you - "too sensitive," "indecisive," "always hardworking," and many others. You've worn this coat for so long that you no longer feel it. This phase is about feeling that coat again - recognizing which fabric pieces were added by others and which truly belong to you.

Main objective: Develop the ability to clearly identify labels and definitions you've accepted from others, understand their origins, and begin questioning whether they truly reflect who you really are.

PHASE 2: REMOVING FALSE IDENTITIES (Days 35-38)

Why this phase next? After identifying labels and definitions that don't truly belong to you, the next step is to actively remove them. This isn't simple - many labels have become so much a part of how you see yourself that abandoning them can feel like losing your identity.

Imagine you're removing layers of old paint from a valuable piece of furniture. Initially, this might make the piece look "empty" or "unfinished." But only by removing those old layers of paint can you see the natural beauty of the wood underneath and create space for something new. Similarly, you must be willing to experience the temporary feeling of "losing" part of your identity to find a more authentic version of yourself.

Main objective: Build the ability to consciously abandon definitions and labels that no longer serve you, no matter how familiar and comfortable they may have become.

PHASE 3: REDEFINING YOURSELF (Days 39-42)

Why is this phase important? After removing old definitions, you have space to explore and determine who you really are - based on internal values, passions, and strengths, not on external expectations or labels.

Think of it as rewriting the script for the play of your life. Previously, this script was written by many different "authors" - parents, friends, teachers, society, media. Now, you'll become the main author. You decide who the main character (yourself) is, what motivates them, and how the story will develop. This is pure creative power - and it belongs entirely to you.

Main objective: Create a new definition of yourself based on core values and internal truths, not based on approval or recognition from others.

PHASE 4: ESTABLISHING YOUR NEW IDENTITY (Days 43-45)

Why end with this phase? Redefining yourself is a breakthrough, but for this change to become sustainable, you need a system to continuously validate yourself without depending on external feedback.

Imagine you've just built a new house. Now you need to establish habits and processes to maintain, care for, and continue beautifying that house over time. Similarly, your new identity needs to be nurtured and continuously reinforced. This phase is about building an internal self-validation system, so you no longer seek validation from outside.

Main objective: Develop specific strategies and habits to continuously self-validate and reinforce your new identity, ensuring it's strong enough to withstand inevitable challenges and doubts.

When you go through all four phases, you won't just abandon old limiting definitions but redefine yourself based on a more solid foundation - one that cannot be shaken by others' opinions or criticism. This isn't an easy journey, but I promise you it's worth every effort. Because at the end of this journey is a version of you that is freer, more authentic, and much stronger.

Day 31: Identity Projection Map

Quick Trigger: "What definitions am I living by that don't truly belong to me?"

Power Question: "What labels have I accepted from others that are limiting me?"

Micro Action (7-10 minutes): Create *an "Identity Projection Map"* - Draw a circle in the middle of a page with your name. Around that circle, write down all the labels and definitions you typically use to describe yourself. For example:

- "I am a perfectionist"
- "I am an extrovert"
- "I'm not good at math"
- "I always have to please everyone"

For each label, draw an arrow indicating its origin:

- Parents/family?
- Friends?
- Society/media?
- Teachers?
- Colleagues?
- Or yourself?

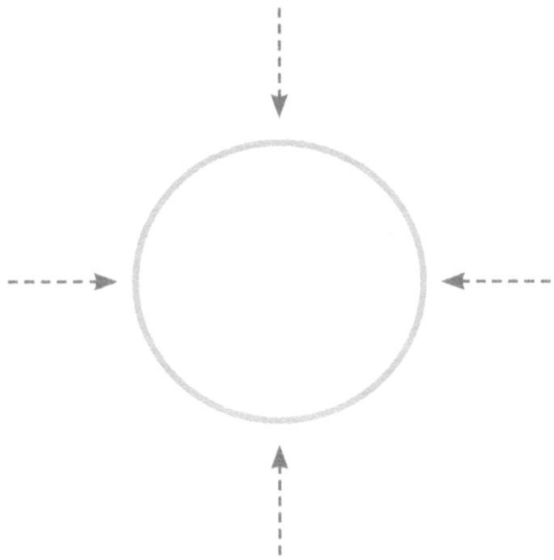

Pro tip: Pay special attention to labels you immediately reject ("I am NOT like that!"). Strong reactions often signal a label you've unconsciously accepted and are trying to prove wrong.

"I am not defined by the labels others assign to me."

Day 32: Hidden Labels Journal

Quick Trigger: "What phrases do I often tell myself that might not be my own?"

Power Question: "Whose critical voice is really in my head?"

Micro Action: Create *a "Hidden Label Journal"* - Over the next 24 hours, pay attention to the self-critical phrases you often tell yourself. Each time you catch one, record:

- The exact phrase ("I'm really bad at communication")
- The physical feeling when thinking it (tension, chest tightness, etc.)
- Whose voice does this sound like from your past?
- When did you first hear this phrase?

After a day, review and circle the 3 phrases that appear most frequently. These are your most powerful "hidden labels" shaping how you see yourself.

The exact phrase	The physical feeling when thinking it	Whose voice does this sound like from your past?	When did you first hear this phrase?

Pro tip: Many critical voices in our heads are actually echoes from others - a strict teacher, a critical relative, or even messages from movies and social media. When you recognize their origins, you can begin to separate them from your true definition of yourself.

"The critical voice in my head is not the truth about me."

Day 33: The "Who Says So?" Investigation

Quick Trigger: "What do I believe about myself that I've never really verified?"

....

....

....

....

....

Power Question: "If no one had ever told me this about myself, what conclusion would I draw on my own?"

....

....

....

....

....

....

Micro Action: Conduct *a "Who Says So Investigation"* - Choose 3 of your strongest beliefs about yourself (both positive and negative) and put them through an investigation:

Write down the belief: "I'm not good at public speaking"

- Ask: "Who told me this? When?"
- Ask: "Is there any actual evidence supporting this belief?"
- Ask: "Is there any evidence that contradicts this belief?"
- Ask: "If I were my own best friend, how would I view this situation?"

1. ....

Ask: ....

Ask: ....

....

Ask: ....

....

2. ....

Ask: ....

Ask: ....

....

Ask: ....

....

3. ....

Ask: ....

Ask: ....

....

Ask: ....

....

Pro tip: Treat beliefs about yourself like scientific hypotheses - needing to be verified with evidence, not just feelings. You'll be surprised to find that many core beliefs about yourself are actually based on very little actual evidence.

"I have the right to question every belief about myself."

Day 34: Chosen vs. Assigned Labels

Quick Trigger: "Which definitions of myself have I actively chosen, and which have I passively accepted?"

Power Question: "If I could completely rewrite the story about myself, which labels would I choose to abandon?"

Micro Action: Create *"Chosen vs. Assigned Labels"* - Draw two columns on a piece of paper:

1. "Assigned labels" - definitions you've passively accepted from others
2. "Chosen labels" - definitions you've actively chosen for yourself

Fill in each column with at least 5 labels. Then, mark the "assigned" labels you want to abandon, and the "chosen" labels you want to strengthen.

Assigned labels	Chosen labels

Pro tip: Pay special attention to positive labels you give yourself but rarely share with others. These are often the most authentic parts of your identity, but may be hidden by insecurity or fear of judgment.

"I have the right to reject definitions I didn't choose."

REMOVING FALSE IDENTITIES

Day 35: Label Removal Challenge

Quick Trigger: "Which label do I feel most compelled to defend when challenged?"

Power Question: "What would happen if I no longer defined myself through that label?"

Micro Action: Write *"Identity Release Statements"* - Choose 5 labels that limit you most from the previous day's exercise. For each label, write a release statement:

- "I am not [label]. I am just a person who has [action/experience] in the past."
- "I am not [label]. That's just a behavior I've chosen, not my essence."

Example: "I am not a 'risk-averse person.' I am just someone who has chosen safety in certain specific situations in the past."

Read each statement aloud and notice the feeling in your body as you say them.

1. ....

....

....

2. ....

....

....

3. ....

....

....

4. ....

....

....

5. ....

....

....

Pro tip: If you feel strong resistance to abandoning a specific label, that's a sign you've invested too much identity in that label. Spend extra time with this label - it might be the key to your biggest breakthrough.

"I am larger and more complex than any single label."

Day 36: Separating Behavior from Identity

Quick Trigger: "How do I confuse what I do with who I am?"

Power Question: "How can I change behaviors without feeling like I'm betraying myself?"

Micro Action: Create *a "Behavior vs. Identity Grid"* - Draw a grid with two columns:

- "Behavior" - things you do
- "Identity" - definitions of who you are

List at least 5 behaviors you regularly engage in that have become part of your definition of yourself. For each behavior, separate it from identity.

Example:

- Behavior: "I often help people when they need it."
- Limiting identity: "I am someone who must always be available for others."
- Separation: "I can choose to help others when it works for me without defining myself as 'someone who must always be available.'"

Behavior	Identity

Separation

Pro tip: Separating behaviors from identity creates space for change and growth. When you no longer define yourself as "I am someone who always X" but instead "Sometimes I choose to X," you're free to experiment with new behaviors without feeling like you're losing yourself.

"My behaviors are choices, not fixed identities."

Day 37: New Identity Experience

Quick Trigger: "Without old labels, how would I act differently?"

Power Question: "What version of me is waiting to be liberated?"

Micro Action: Conduct *an "Identity Experimentation"* - Choose one limiting label you want to abandon (e.g., "I'm not good at talking to strangers"). For the next 24 hours, try living as if that label doesn't exist:

1. Write a new temporary definition: "Today, I am someone comfortable chatting with strangers."
2. Identify a small action aligned with the new definition (start a conversation with a store clerk, offer an opinion in a meeting)
3. Take that action
4. Record: How did it feel? How did others react? What did you learn?

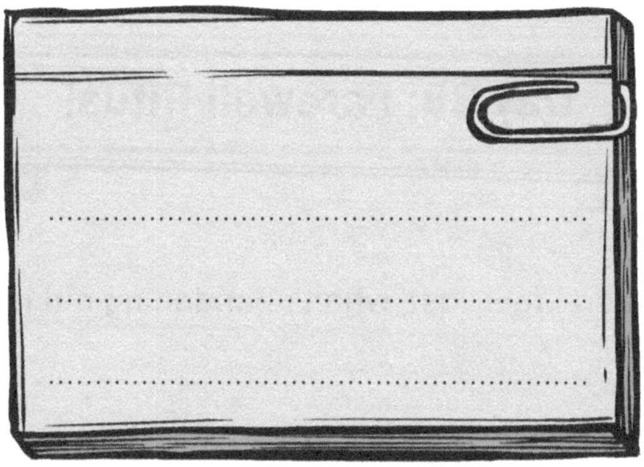

Write a new temporary definition:

Identify a small action:

Record: How did it feel? How did others react? What did you learn?

Pro tip: Don't think of this as "pretending to be someone else." Instead, see it as exploring a part of you that has always existed but was hidden by limiting labels. You're not becoming someone different - you're exploring your whole self.

"I can experiment with new identities anytime."

Day 38: Farewell Ritual

Quick Trigger: "What do I feel 'lost' when abandoning old labels?"

Power Question: "How can I honor the past while still moving forward?"

Micro Action: Create *a "Letting Go Ceremony"* - Choose one label you're ready to completely abandon. Perform a farewell ritual:

1. Write the label on a piece of paper
2. Write:
   - "This label served me by..." (identify the benefits it provided)
   - "I no longer need this label because..." (reasons you've outgrown it)
   - "To replace it, I now choose..." (better new definition)
3. Perform a symbolic action: tear up the paper, burn it (safely), or bury it.
4. Say aloud: "I appreciate the lesson, but now I'm ready to continue."

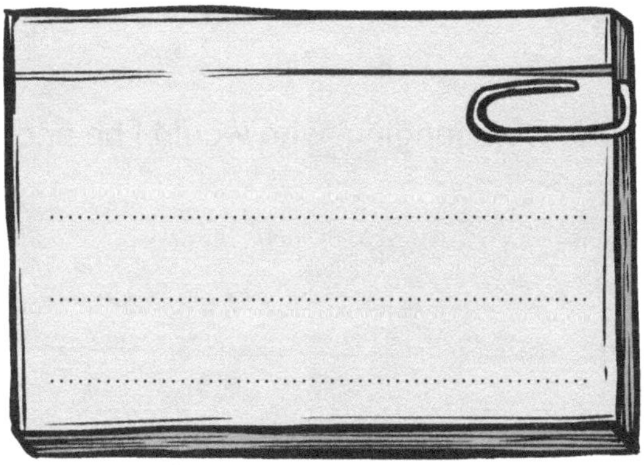

Pro tip: Rituals have amazing power in marking transitions. Our brains respond to symbolic actions in ways that reason alone cannot achieve. Don't skip this step even if it seems strange - symbolism creates real changes in the mind.

"I can experiment with new identities anytime."

PHASE 03 REDEFINING YOURSELF

Day 39: Core Values Map

Quick Trigger: "If no one were judging, who would I be and what would I do?"

....

....

....

Power Question: "What core values truly define who I am?"

....

....

....

....

Micro Action: Create a *"Core Values Map"* - On a blank piece of paper, write answers to these questions:

1. "What makes me feel most alive?"
2. "When do I feel most satisfied and proud of myself?"
3. "What qualities do I admire in others?"
4. "What makes me feel angry or sad when I see it in the world?"
5. "If I didn't have to worry about money or approval, what would I spend time on?"

From your answers, identify 3-5 core values (like: freedom, creativity, compassion, integrity, curiosity...) that truly matter to you.

....

....

....

....

....

....

....

....

....

....

....

....

Pro tip: Pay attention to values that energize you when you think about them. If a value feels like a "should" or "ought to," it might be an imposed value rather than your true value.

"My core values guide me more powerfully than any label."

Day 40: Value-Based Identity Statement

Quick Trigger: "How can I build an identity based on values rather than achievements?"

Power Question: "How do I want to be remembered when I'm no longer in this world?"

Micro Action: Create *a "Value-Based Identity Statement"* - Using the core values from the previous day, write a statement about yourself (about 100-150 words) beginning with:

"I am someone who defines myself through [value 1], [value 2], and [value 3]. This means that I..."

Write about how these values manifest in your daily life, not through achievements or status, but through how you interact with the world and those around you.

Read this statement aloud and adjust until it feels completely right for you.

....

....

....

....

....

....

....

....

....

....

....

Pro tip: When writing this statement, avoid all forms of "I must" or "I should." Instead, focus on "I choose" and "I commit." This seemingly small difference creates a major change in how you experience your identity - from obligation to active choice.

"I am becoming, shaped by values rather than expectations."

Day 41: Creating New History

Quick Trigger: "What stories do I often tell about myself?"

Power Question: "How can I rewrite my personal narrative in a more empowering way?"

Micro Action: Conduct *a "Story Reframing Exercise"* - Choose a story you often tell about yourself (or tell yourself) that is limiting in nature. For example: "I always procrastinate everything until the last minute."

Rewrite this story from three different perspectives:

1. Learning perspective: "I am learning to manage my time more effectively."
2. Growth perspective: "I have grown from someone who does everything at the last minute to someone who appreciates planning ahead."
3. Strength perspective: "My ability to work under pressure has helped me succeed in emergency situations."

Choose the version of the story that feels most right and commit to telling that version instead of the old one.

....

....

....

....

....

....

....

....

....

Pro tip: We often don't realize that the "truth" about ourselves is largely the story we choose to tell. Two people can experience the same event and build completely different stories from it. Reframing isn't lying - it's choosing the most empowering frame that's still honest to your experience.

"I am becoming, shaped by values rather than expectations."

Day 42: New Identity Reflection

Quick Trigger: "How do I feel about the new identity that's forming?"

Power Question: "What will be different in my life when I fully embrace this new identity?"

Micro Action: Create *a "New Identity Reflection"* - Spend 20-30 minutes in free writing to explore feelings about your emerging new identity. Answer:

1. "Three things I'm beginning to realize about my true self are..."
2. "I feel [emotion] when thinking about abandoning old definitions because..."
3. "I feel [emotion] when thinking about living by my new identity because..."
4. "Three specific changes people might notice when I live true to this new identity are..."
5. "The hardest thing about maintaining this new identity will be... and I will cope by..."

....

....

....

....

....

....

....

....

....

....

....

Pro tip: As humans, we often feel conflicted about change - even positive change. You might simultaneously feel excited about your new identity and anxious about abandoning the old one. This is completely normal! Embrace this ambivalence and recognize it as a natural part of the transition process.

"I am becoming the most authentic version of myself."

PHASE 04 ESTABLISHING YOUR NEW IDENTITY

Day 43: Building a Self-Validation System

Quick Trigger: "Whose approval do I still depend on?"

Power Question: "How can I validate myself without needing external approval?"

Micro Action: Develop *a "Self-Validation Protocol"* - Create a system to validate your inherent worth without depending on others' opinions:

1. Identify 3 situations where you typically seek external validation (feedback on work, appearance, decisions)
2. For each situation, write:
   - Self-assessment question: "Does this align with my core values?"
   - Self-validation statement: "I'm proud that I..."
   - Self-care action: a small action to reward yourself

Commit to using this protocol 3 times in the coming week before seeking approval from others.

1. ....

Self-assessment question: ....

....

Self-validation statement: ....

....

Self-care action: ....

....

1. ....

Self-assessment question: ....

....

Self-validation statement: ....

....

Self-care action: ....

....

1. ....

Self-assessment question: ....

....

Self-validation statement: ....

....

Self-care action: ....

....

Pro tip: Self-validation doesn't mean ignoring all external feedback. Instead, it means you first evaluate yourself by internal standards, then consider outside opinions - and only from people aligned with your values.

"The only approval I need is my own."

Day 44: Embodied Identity

Quick Trigger: "How will I introduce my new self to others?"

Power Question: "How can I live true to my new identity without explaining or justifying?"

Micro Action: Create *an "Identity Embodiment Practice"* - Design 3 specific ways to begin embodying your new identity in daily life:

1. A change in how you introduce yourself
2. A change in your physical space (decor, clothing, objects)
3. A change in your daily habits or activities

Commit to implementing at least one of these changes in the next 48 hours.

Example: If your core value is "creativity," you might:

- Introduction: "I'm someone exploring creative ways to [your field]"
- Space: Add a creative corner to your home or office
- Habit: Spend 15 minutes daily free writing/drawing/creating

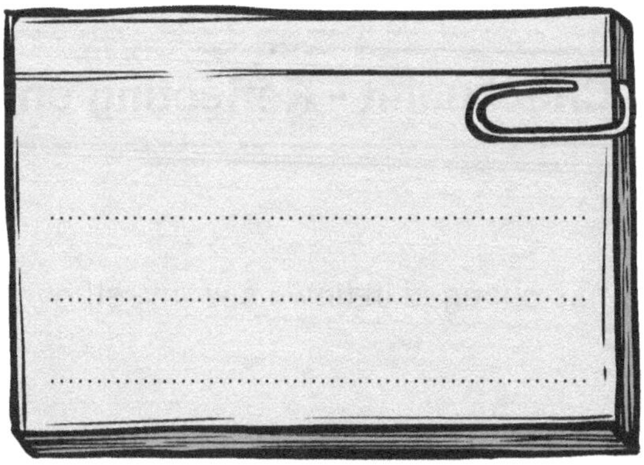

1. ....

....

....

2. ....

....

....

3. ....

....

....

Pro tip: Small, tangible changes often have a big impact on how we feel about ourselves. Our brains take physical actions as evidence for new beliefs. Each time you act in alignment with your new identity, you reinforce it more powerfully than merely thinking about it could.

"I don't need to explain my true identity - I just need to live it."

Day 45: Checkpoint - Reflecting on Stage 3

Quick Trigger: "What has changed in how I see myself over the past 15 days?"

....

....

....

....

....

Power Question: "What have I learned about redefining myself independent of others' opinions?"

....

....

....

....

Micro Action: Create *an "Identity Embodiment Practice"* - Design 3 specific ways to begin embodying your new identity in daily life:

1. Spend 30 minutes deeply reflecting on the entire Stage 3 journey
2. Reread all your notes and completed exercises
3. Write down:
   - 3 limiting labels you've abandoned
   - 3 core values you've identified
   - 3 ways you've begun living by your new identity
4. Create a specific commitment to continue building and reinforcing your new identity over the next 30 days

Pro tip: The process of redefining yourself isn't a one-time event - it's a lifelong journey. Don't expect to feel completely "transformed" after 15 days. Instead, view this as planting seeds that will continue to grow for years to come. Each time you choose an identity based on values rather than external labels, that seed grows stronger.

"I am the author of my life story, not a supporting character in someone else's."

BONUS SECTION: BODY SOVEREIGNTY & SELF-WORTH (ESPECIALLY FOR WOMEN)

Exercise 1: My Body, My Timeline

Quick Trigger: "How do I compare my body/progress with others?"

....

....

....

....

....

Power Question: "How can I honor my body's unique journey?"

....

....

....

....

....

....

Micro Action: Create *a "Personal Body Timeline"* - On a piece of paper, draw a timeline of your relationship with your body:

1. Mark 5-7 significant moments from childhood to present
2. For each moment, write:
   - How you felt about your body
   - Who/what influenced that feeling
   - A message you now want to send to yourself at that time
3. End the timeline with an empowering statement about your body in the present and future

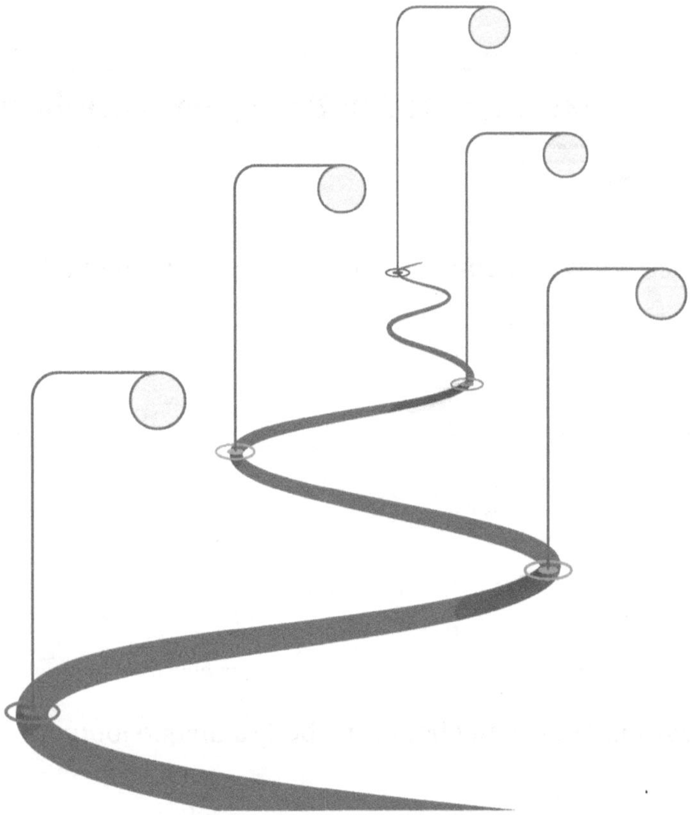

Pro tip: Pay attention to times when your relationship with your body shifted - especially from positive to negative. These moments often mark when you internalized external standards. Identifying the source of these standards can help you begin to release them.

"My body has its own schedule and journey, not needing to be like anyone else's."

Exercise 2: Worth Beyond Image

Quick Trigger: "How much does my self-worth depend on appearance?"

Power Question: "How can I build a solid sense of worth independent of external image?"

Micro Action: Create *a "Non-Image Worth Inventory"* - Create a comprehensive list of your value beyond appearance:

1. List 10 qualities, talents, or contributions unrelated to appearance
2. For each item, write a specific example of how it enriches your life or others'
3. Identify 3-5 qualities you want to develop further in the future
4. Write a commitment to invest more in these aspects of yourself

Qualities/ Talents/ Contributions	Example

Pro tip: Challenge yourself to view people in your life similarly - evaluating them based on inner qualities, not appearance. This not only reinforces your new view of yourself but also enriches your relationships.

"My worth exists deep within,
independent of outward appearance."

Mini-Milestone 03

CONGRATULATIONS! You've completed Stage 3 of the journey!

Take a moment to recognize the extraordinary achievement you've accomplished:

- You've identified labels that don't truly belong to you
- You've had the courage to remove labels that have defined you for years
- You've redefined yourself based on core values, not external expectations
- You've developed a self-validation system independent of others' approval

To acknowledge this journey, complete the following sentence and record it in your journal:

"I have abandoned ________________________ limiting labels and begun building a new identity based on ____ core values."

Example: "I have abandoned the label 'people pleaser' and begun building a new identity based on the core values of freedom, integrity, and compassion."

In the upcoming Stage 4, we'll learn how to turn all this inner work into concrete action in the world - how to create meaningful impact based on your authentic identity.

Remember: "Authentic identity isn't a destination, but a continuous journey. Each day, you have the opportunity to decide: Will I live by the labels assigned to me, or will I write my own definition?"

Share your journey: If you feel comfortable, share one core value you've discovered over the past 15 days on social media with the hashtag #LetThemTalkLetMeBuild. By sharing your journey, you may inspire others to begin a similar one.

STAGE 04

LET ME BUILD

LET ME BUILD

LET ME BUILD

Creating Your Own Reality

01 02 03 04 05 06 07 08 09 10 11 12 13 14 15 16 17 18 19 20

21 22 23 24 25 26 27 28 29 30 31 32 33 34 35 36 37 38 39 40

41 42 43 44 45 46 47 48 49 50 51 52 53 54 55 56 57 58 59 60

Dear friend,

WOW – looking back at the journey you've traveled, it's amazing! In Stage 1, you learned to stop worrying about others' opinions. In Stage 2, you built an impenetrable focus space. In Stage 3, you redefined your authentic identity. Now, we enter the final and most important stage – where everything converges.

Here's the truth: Not caring about others' opinions, protecting your focus, and understanding yourself is NOT ENOUGH. That's just the foundation. Now, you need to use that foundation to build something – to create the reality you actually want to live.

Imagine you've just learned how to escape from the mental prison – the place where you constantly worried about others' opinions. Now you're free. But free to do what? This is exactly the question that Stage 4 will help you answer.

In the coming days, we'll shift from *"reacting to judgment"* to *"proactively creating."* We'll build mechanisms, systems, and skills so you not only escape the influence of others' opinions, but actively construct a life that reflects your core values and authentic vision.

This isn't about *"success"* in the traditional definition. This is about living a SOVEREIGN life – where you, not society, define what success means for you.

Our secret weapons: Reality Creation Protocol™ combined with Inner Sovereignty Framework™

Reality Creation Protocol™ is a method I developed after working with people who had overcome the fear of judgment but still didn't know what to do next. Combined with **Inner Sovereignty Framework™**, this is a powerful system that helps you:

1. Create an authentic vision untainted by social expectations
2. Build a decision-making system based on core values
3. Develop the ability to maintain your path when facing criticism
4. Design a life that reflects who you really are, not the version others want you to become

How is this different from previous stages? Stages 1-3 focused on FREEING you from the influence of others' opinions. Stage 4 focuses on what you'll do with that freedom – how to BUILD an authentic life based on your new foundation.

Let's begin this final building journey.

Overview of the 4 Phases

Before we begin, let's understand more about the "map" we'll follow in these final 15 days. Each phase is designed to build upon the previous one, similar to constructing a building - from designing blueprints to laying foundations, erecting the frame, and finishing the house. Let's examine in more detail why we've arranged this journey this way:

PHASE 1: UNINFLUENCED VISION (Days 46-49)

Why start here? Before you can build anything, you need to know what you want to build. But here's the challenge: Most of our "dreams" have been so deeply influenced by social expectations that we're no longer sure what our true aspirations are.

Imagine you've spent your entire life looking at the world through colored glasses. You've become so accustomed to everything having certain colors that when you finally remove the glasses, the true colors of the world might overwhelm you. Similarly, when you remove the "others' opinions" filter from your vision, you might not immediately recognize your true aspirations. This phase helps you gradually see and trust your authentic vision.

Main objective: Develop a clear vision of the life you truly want to build, based on your real values and aspirations, uninfluenced by social expectations or fear of judgment.

PHASE 2: BUILDING AUTONOMOUS SYSTEMS (Days 50-53)

Why this phase next? With a clear vision, the next step is building systems that help you maintain that path, even when facing opposition. This is when we create a new "operating system" for your life - a decision-making system based on core values instead of reacting to external pressures.

Think of it as building a personal Global Positioning System (GPS). Instead of relying on road signs and others' opinions to know where you should go, you have an internal system that always guides you back to your true path. This system will help you navigate even when there's fog (doubt) or detours (criticism).

Main objective: Develop a solid decision-making system based on your core values that helps you maintain your authentic direction even when facing external pressure.

PHASE 3: SKILLS FOR FACING CHALLENGES (Days 54-57)

Why is this phase important? The truth is, even with a clear vision and solid system, you'll still face opposition. Others will challenge, criticize, or even try to sabotage your path. This phase equips you with specific skills to handle these challenges without being defeated or deflected.

Imagine you're the captain of a ship. You have a map (vision) and a compass (decision-making system), but you still need to know how to navigate through storms. This phase teaches you how to steer your ship through storms of criticism, doubt, and opposition to reach your destination.

Main objective: Develop specific strategies and response scripts to maintain your path when facing opposition, while protecting the mental space you've created in previous stages.

PHASE 4: AUTHENTIC LIVING SYSTEMS (Days 58-60)

Why end with this phase? The final days of the 60-day journey will focus on synthesizing everything you've learned to create an overall blueprint for your authentic life - a detailed plan that will continue to guide you long after the program ends.

Picture this as when you look back at the entire structure you've built - walls, roof, windows, doors - and ensure everything works together as a unified system. Not just ensuring everything works now, but also planning for this house to continue standing strong and growing for years to come.

Main objective: Create a comprehensive blueprint for your authentic life, integrating all tools and strategies from the past 60 days into a sustainable living system for the long term.

When you go through all four phases, you won't just complete the 60-day journey - you'll begin a new journey of a life designed and built on YOUR terms. You won't just know how to avoid being influenced by others' opinions; you'll have the skills and systems to proactively build a life that reflects your authentic values and vision. This is the final and most precious achievement of the entire program.

PHASE 01

UNINFLUENCED VISION

Day 46: Abandoned Dreams Survey

Quick Trigger: "What dreams have I abandoned because I was afraid of what others would think?"

Power Question: "If no one were judging, what would I truly want to create in my life?"

Micro Action: Create *an "Abandoned Dreams Inventory"* - Spend 20 minutes writing down all the dreams, aspirations, or projects you've abandoned or never pursued because of:

- Fear of what others would think
- Worry about criticism or being ridiculed
- Feeling it was "unrealistic" or "selfish"
- Not wanting to upset or disappoint others

After listing them, mark the 3 dreams that still evoke strong emotions when you think about them. For each dream, write:

- "What I really want is ___"
- "I abandoned this because ___"
- "A smaller version I could still pursue is ___"

1. ....

....

....

....

....

2. ....

....

....

....

....

3. ....

....

....

....

....

Pro tip: Pay attention to dreams that make you feel embarrassed or silly when thinking about them. Shame is often a sign of an authentic aspiration that's been buried under layers of social judgment. These may be the most important dreams to re-explore.

"My dreams don't need permission from others."

Day 47: Breaking Success Templates

Quick Trigger: "Whose definition of 'success' am I trying to achieve?"

Power Question: "If I could define success for myself, what would it look like?"

Micro Action: Create *a "Success Template Disruption"* - Split a piece of paper in half:

1. Left side: "Imposed success definitions" - list everything you feel you must achieve to be considered "successful" (money, position, possessions, marriage, etc.)

2. Right side: "Authentic success definitions" - write how you would define success if no one were watching

For each item in the "imposed" column, ask yourself:

- "Who taught me this was important?"
- "Does this actually matter to ME?"
- "If no one knew I achieved this, would it still be important?"

Imposed success definitions		Authentic success definitions
	→	
	→	
	→	
	→	
	→	

Pro tip: A sign to recognize whether a goal is truly yours: When you imagine achieving it without anyone knowing or being impressed, do you still feel it's valuable? Or is it only valuable when recognized by others? Goals that are only valuable when recognized are often signs of aspirations that aren't truly yours.

"I refuse to pursue success I don't actually want."

Day 48: Exploring Hidden Success

Quick Trigger: "How do I see myself happy and successful?"

Power Question: "What version of success aligns with my authentic values?"

Micro Action: Create *an "Alternative Success Visualization"* - Conduct a guided imagination exercise:

1. Find a quiet space, sit comfortably, and close your eyes

2. Imagine meeting a future version of yourself - someone living a happy, fulfilling life according to YOUR definition

3. Observe and record (after finishing the visualization):
   - What is future-you doing every day?
   - What does future-you's living space look like?
   - Who does future-you spend time with?
   - When does future-you look happiest?
   - What is future-you most proud of?

4. Write down 3-5 most surprising elements about this future life - things that might differ from what you're currently pursuing

Pro tip: If you find it difficult to imagine a future different from the "script" you've been following, try the "inversion technique": Imagine all the things society says are important suddenly become unimportant. Money? Not important. Position? Not important. Status? Not important. In that world, what would you choose to do with your life?

"My authentic success might look completely different from what I've been taught to pursue."

Day 49: Authentic Vision Board

Quick Trigger: "What do I truly want to build in my life?"

Power Question: "How can I continuously connect with my authentic vision?"

Micro Action: Develop *an "Authentic Vision Board"* - Create a vision board (physical or digital) based entirely on internal aspirations:

1. Gather images, words, and symbols representing your authentic vision (from previous exercises)

2. When placing each element on the board, ask yourself: "Is this truly what I want, or what I feel I should want?"

3. For each element you decide to keep, write a short sentence explaining WHY it matters to you in a personal and authentic way

4. Place this board where you'll see it daily

Pro tip: Traditional vision boards are often full of symbols of success according to social definitions (expensive cars, big houses, etc.). Challenge yourself to create a board without any status quo symbols unless they truly evoke excitement and meaning for YOU. If that means your board has fewer material images and more symbols of experiences, emotions, or contributions, that's perfectly fine!

"Every day I build MY vision, not someone else's."

PHASE 02

BUILDING AUTONOMOUS SYSTEMS

Day 50: Values Compass

Quick Trigger: "What do I usually base my decisions on?"

Power Question: "How can I use my core values as a compass for every decision?"

Micro Action: Create *a "Values Compass"* - Develop a decision-making guide based on values:

1. On a piece of paper, list the 3-5 core values identified in Stage 3
2. For each value, write:
   - Specific definition of this value FOR YOU
   - 3 signs that you're living according to this value
   - 3 warning signs that you're deviating from this value
3. Create 3-5 guiding questions to ask yourself when making important decisions, for example:
   - "Does this decision bring me closer to ____ [value]?"
   - "Can I make this decision in a way that expresses ____ [value]?"

1. ....

....

....

1: ....

2: ....

3: ....

1: ....

2: ....

3: ....

2. ....

....

....

1: ....

2: ....

3: ....

1: ....

2: ....

3: ....

3. ....

....

....

1: ....

2: ....

3: ....

1: ....

2: ....

3: ....

4. ....

....

....

1: ....

2: ....

3: ....

1: ....

2: ....

3: ....

5. ....

....

....

1: ....

2: ....

3: ....

1: ....

2: ....

3: ....

Question 1:..

....

Question 2:..

....

Question 3:..

....

Question 4:..

....

Question 5:..

....

Pro tip: To make this tool habitual, practice with small decisions too. Before deciding where to eat dinner, what movie to watch, or how to spend an evening, quickly run through your values compass. This helps create a "decision-making muscle" based on values that will serve you when facing bigger decisions.

"My values are my most reliable compass."

Day 51: Pressure Journal

Quick Trigger: "Whose reactions still affect me the most?"

Power Question: "How can I recognize when I'm deciding based on pressure rather than values?"

Micro Action: Create *a "Pressure Journal"* - Over the next 24 hours, track every time you feel pressure to decide or act in a way that doesn't truly align with you:

1. Record:
   - Specific situation or decision
   - Source of pressure (specific person, group, social media, etc.)
   - Physical sensations (tension where? racing heart? difficulty breathing?)
2. What you actually want vs. what you feel you should do
3. For each situation, write a short values-based response: "Based on my values, I would..."

PRESSURE JOURNAL – 24-HOUR REFLECTION TABLE

Time of Situation	Specific Situation or Decision	Source of Pressure	Physical Sensations	What I Truly Want	What I Feel I "Should" Do	Values-Based Response

Pro tip: Pay special attention to your body's sensations! Your body often recognizes when you're being pressured before your mind does. Tight neck? Tense shoulders? Stomach knots? These sensations can be an "early warning system" that you're making decisions based on external pressure, not internal values.

"I recognize pressure and choose my values instead."

Day 52: Value-Based Decision Matrix

Quick Trigger: "How can I structure my decision-making process according to my values?"

....

....

....

....

Power Question: "What system can I create to ensure every decision reflects who I truly am?"

....

....

....

....

Micro Action: Build *a "Value-Based Decision Matrix"* - Create a decision matrix based on your core values:

1. Draw a table with your core values along the top
2. At each intersection, create a value-based question to evaluate decisions, for example:
   - For "Freedom" value: "Does this decision create more space and freedom in my life?"
   - For "Creativity" value: "Does this decision allow me to express creativity in meaningful ways?"
3. Create a 1-10 scale to evaluate each decision based on how it reflects each value
   - 1-3: Contradicts this value 4-6: Neutral
   - 7-8: Aligns quite well 9-10: Perfectly aligns
4. Test the matrix with a decision you're currently considering

SET UP THE MATRIX FRAMEWORK

CORE VALUES	EVALUATION QUESTIONS

DEFINE YOUR DECISION

Decision I'm considering: ....

....

OPTIONS	VALUE 1	VALUE 2	VALUE 3	VALUE 4	TOTAL SCORE
	....../10	....../10	....../10	....../10	
	....../10	....../10	....../10	....../10	
	....../10	....../10	....../10	....../10	

Decision I'm considering: ....

....

OPTIONS	VALUE 1	VALUE 2	VALUE 3	VALUE 4	TOTAL SCORE
	....../10	....../10	....../10	....../10	
	....../10	....../10	....../10	....../10	
	....../10	....../10	....../10	....../10	

....

....

....

....

Pro tip: Not all values are equally important for every decision. When using this matrix, you can also assign weights to values based on their relevance to the specific decision. Some decisions might relate more to "freedom" than "connection," and vice versa. Recognizing this makes your matrix more flexible and accurate.

"Every decision is an opportunity to express my authentic values."

Day 53: Inner Sovereignty System

Quick Trigger: "How do I maintain autonomy when facing external pressure?"

Power Question: "How can I build a life system that's completely decided by me?"

Micro Action: Create *an "Inner Sovereignty System"* - Develop a decision-making process that protects your inner integrity:

1. Identify 3-5 specific "Alert States" - signs that you might be giving up your autonomy (e.g., feeling pressure to respond immediately, feeling confused and uncertain, etc.)
2. For each alert state, develop a 3-step process to regain autonomy:
   - Step 1: Immediate action to create space (e.g., "I need to think about this. I'll respond later.")
   - Step 2: Recovery process (e.g., 5 minutes of meditation, 3 deep breaths, short walk)
   - Step 3: Values-oriented question (from your values compass)
3. Create a small "autonomy card" with alert states and processes to carry with you

INNER SOVEREIGNTY SYSTEM TABLE

Warning Sign (Inner Alarm)	Step 1: Immediate Space-Creating Action	Step 2: Recovery Ritual	Step 3: Value-Based Reflection Question
e.g. Feeling pressured to respond immediately when not ready	"I need time to think. I'll get back to you later."	3 deep breaths + step away from screen for 5 minutes	"If I choose based on my inner freedom, how would I respond?"

Pro tip: Practice "minimum response time" for all requests or decisions. Even if it's just 5 minutes, stepping back and confirming that your response aligns with your values can make a huge difference. This is especially important for people who tend to respond quickly to please others or avoid conflict.

"I can pause anytime to ensure my decisions are my own."

PHASE 03

SKILLS FOR FACING CHALLENGES

Day 54: Trigger Map

Quick Trigger: "What reactions from others still make me waver?"

....

....

....

....

....

Power Question: "How can I prepare in advance for the negative reactions I might encounter?"

....

....

....

....

....

....

Micro Action: Create *a "Trigger Map"* - Map out reactions from others that could make you abandon your authentic vision:

1. Write your vision or authentic goal in the center of a page
2. Around it, write all possible negative reactions from others (criticism, doubt, etc.)
3. For each reaction, rate from 1-10 how likely it is to derail you
4. For the 3 highest-scoring reactions, write specific value-based responses:
    - "When others say ___, I will remember that ___"
    - "Instead of doubting myself, I will ___"

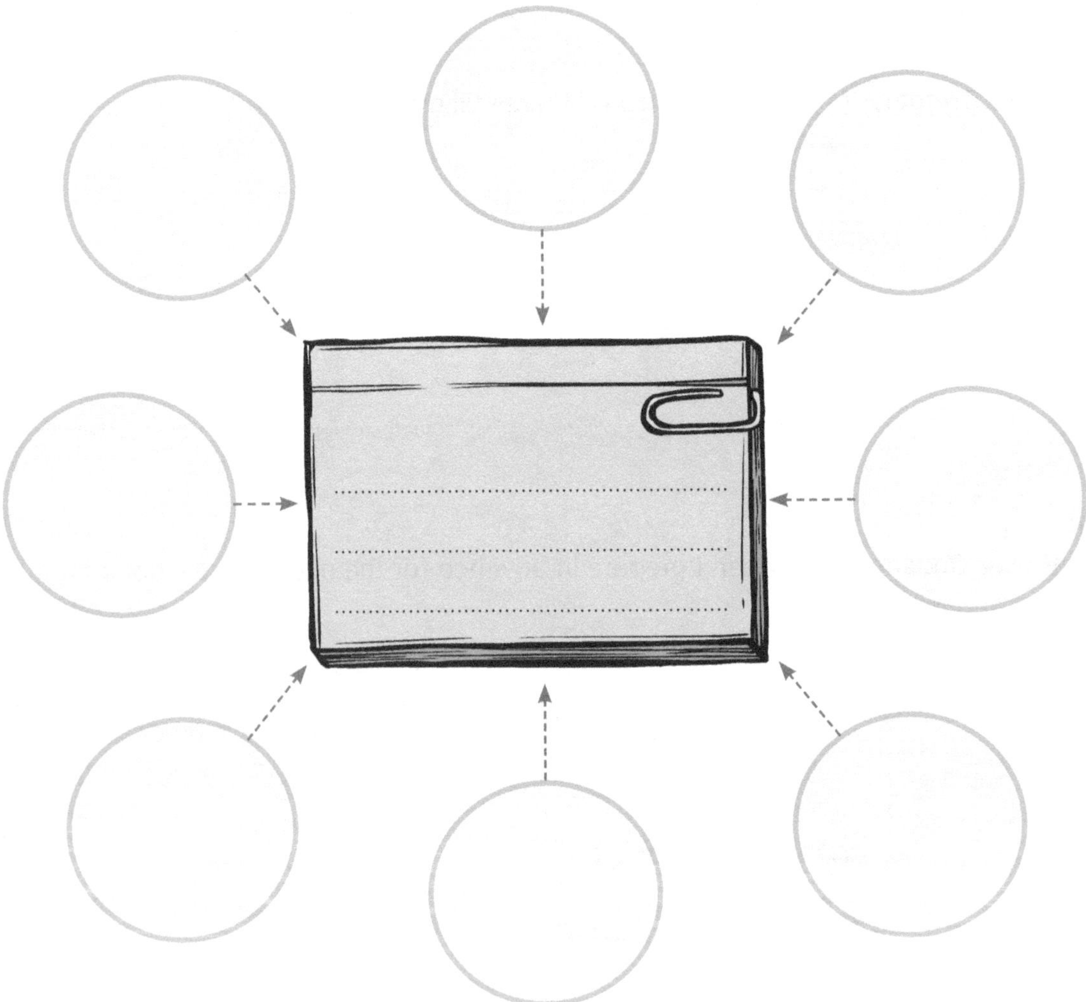

1. ....

....

....

....

....

....

2. ....

....

....

....

....

3. ....

....

....

....

....

Pro tip: Visualization is a powerful tool. Spend time clearly imagining yourself receiving each negative reaction, feeling the emotion, and then imagining yourself responding calmly with your prepared response. This mental rehearsal creates new neural pathways in the brain, helping your actual response be calmer and more proactive when the situation really occurs.

"I can't control others' reactions, but I can prepare for them."

Day 55: Resilience Response Scripts

Quick Trigger: "How do I usually react when criticized or opposed?"

....

....

....

....

Power Question: "How can I maintain my vision when criticized or opposed?"

....

....

....

....

Micro Action: Develop *"Resilience Response Scripts"* - Write response scripts for common challenging situations:

1. Identify 5 challenging situations you might face when pursuing your authentic vision:
   - Direct criticism
   - Doubt or mockery
   - Worry or fear from loved ones
   - Passive opposition (lack of support)
   - Guilt trips from others
2. For each situation, develop a response script with 3 parts:
   - Acknowledgment: "I understand you're feeling/thinking..."
   - Boundary: "However, this is my decision/path..."
   - Invitation/Exit: "If you want to support me, you can..." OR "I appreciate your concern, but I'm not looking for advice about this."
3. Practice saying these scripts aloud

1. ....

Acknowledgment: ....

....

....

Boundary: ....

....

....

Invitation/Exit: ....

....

....

2. ....

Acknowledgment: ....

....

....

Boundary: ....

....

....

Invitation/Exit: ....

....

....

3. ....

Acknowledgment: ....

....

....

Boundary: ....

....

....

Invitation/Exit: ....

....

....

4. ....

Acknowledgment: ....

....

....

Boundary: ....

....

....

Invitation/Exit: ....

....

....

5. ....

Acknowledgment: ....

....

....

Boundary: ....

....

....

Invitation/Exit: ....

....

....

Pro tip: Tone and body language play crucial roles. When practicing scripts, ensure you maintain a calm and confident voice, stand straight, and maintain eye contact. If possible, practice in front of a mirror or record yourself to see whether you're projecting confidence or insecurity.

"I can stay firm in my position
without being defensive or compromising."

Day 56: Inner Critic Dialogue

Quick Trigger: "What does my inner critic say when I pursue my authentic vision?"

Power Question: "How can I transform self-criticism into useful feedback?"

Micro Action: Conduct *an "Inner Critic Dialogue"* - Engage in a purposeful conversation with the critical voice inside you:

1. On a page, start writing down all the worries, fears, and criticisms your inner voice says about your vision/dreams
2. For each criticism, write responses with three types of questions:
    - Reality questions: "Is there any actual evidence for this?"
    - Empowerment questions: "Even if there are challenges, how can I handle them?"
    - Values-oriented questions: "What aligns best with my values in this situation?"
3. After each round of responses, record any changes in your emotions or thoughts

1. ....

Reality questions: ....

....

Empowerment questions: ....

....

Values-oriented questions: ....

....

....

Changes in your emotions or thoughts: ....

....

....

2. ....

Reality questions: ....

....

Empowerment questions: ....

....

Values-oriented questions: ....

....

....

Changes in your emotions or thoughts: ....

....

....

3. ....

Reality questions: ....

....

Empowerment questions: ....

....

Values-oriented questions: ....

....

....

Changes in your emotions or thoughts: ....

....

....

Pro tip: Instead of trying to silence your inner critic (which rarely works), treat them like an overly worried advisor who might have some valid points but often exaggerates risks and ignores your capabilities. Gentle but firm respect, along with thoughtful questions, is often more effective than fighting against or ignoring them.

"I am in charge of my inner dialogue."

Day 57: Discomfort Tolerance Practice

Quick Trigger: "How do I usually react to discomfort when pursuing my goals?"

Power Question: "How can I expand my ability to tolerate discomfort without giving up?"

Micro Action: Conduct *"Discomfort Tolerance Practice"* - Build your ability to stay in discomfort with a progressive challenge:

1. Choose a relatively harmless but uncomfortable activity you can do for 10 minutes (cold shower, holding a plank, sitting in meditation in an uncomfortable position, etc.)
2. Before starting, set intention and write down:
   - "I am choosing this, no one is forcing me to do it"
   - "Discomfort is not a sign of danger or wrongness"
   - "I can feel discomfort without having to act immediately"

3. Throughout the activity, practice:

- Observing discomfort without judgment
- Noticing the urge to stop or change
- Continuing despite discomfort (unless there's actual pain)

3. Afterward, record:

- What you noticed about the discomfort
- How you overcame the urge to stop
- How this exercise might apply to facing discomfort when pursuing your authentic vision

Ativity: ....

....

....

....

....

....

....

....

....

....

....

....

....

....

Pro tip: The ability to tolerate discomfort is a skill that can be trained like a muscle. Start with small challenges and gradually increase. Each time you stay in discomfort without reacting immediately, you're expanding your "tolerance zone" - which will be invaluable when you face the discomfort of being criticized or doubted while pursuing your vision.

"I can feel discomfort without being controlled by it."

PHASE 04

AUTHENTIC LIVING SYSTEMS

Day 58: Reality Check System

Quick Trigger: "How do I know I'm still on the right track?"

Power Question: "What checkpoints can I establish to ensure I'm still living according to my authentic values and vision?"

Micro Action: Design *a "Reality Check System"* - Create a regular check-in system to ensure you're still living authentically:

1. Develop three types of checkpoints:
   - Daily check (3-5 quick questions you'll ask yourself each evening)
   - Weekly check (deeper reflection, 20-30 minutes)
   - Monthly check (comprehensive evaluation with specific questions about living according to values)
2. For each type, write:
   - Specific questions you'll ask yourself
   - Process you'll follow
   - How you'll record and track answers
3. Set up reminder systems on your phone/calendar to ensure you do each type of check

DAILY CHECK

Quick questions 1: ....

....

....

....

Quick questions 2: ....

....

....

....

Quick questions 3: ....

....

....

....

Quick questions 4: ....

....

....

....

Quick questions 5: ....

....

....

....

WEEKLY CHECK

Quick questions 1: ....

....

....

....

....

....

Quick questions 2: ....

....

....

....

....

....

Quick questions 3: ....

MONTHLY CHECK

Pro tip: The secret to maintaining a check-in system is making it easy and even enjoyable. If the process is too complex or time-consuming, you might skip it. Think of ways to make this a pleasant routine - perhaps by combining it with a favorite drink, special music, or sitting in a favorite location.

"Regular check-ins help me maintain my authentic direction."

Day 59: Journey Integration Overview

Quick Trigger: "What have I learned in the past 59 days?"

....

....

....

....

Power Question: "How can I integrate all these tools and lessons into a unified living system?"

....

....

....

....

Micro Action: Create *a "Journey Integration Map"* - Build a visual map to connect and integrate everything you've learned:

1. On a large piece of paper, draw four sections corresponding to the four stages:
    - Stage 1: Let Them Talk (Freedom from others' opinions)
    - Stage 2: Let Me Focus (Building focus space)
    - Stage 3: Let Me Grow (Redefining identity)
    - Stage 4: Let Me Build (Creating your own reality)
2. In each section, write:
    - 3 most powerful tools/exercises from that stage
    - How these tools connect to other stages
    - How you'll continue using these tools
3. Draw connecting lines between tools and exercises across stages, creating an integrated "ecosystem"

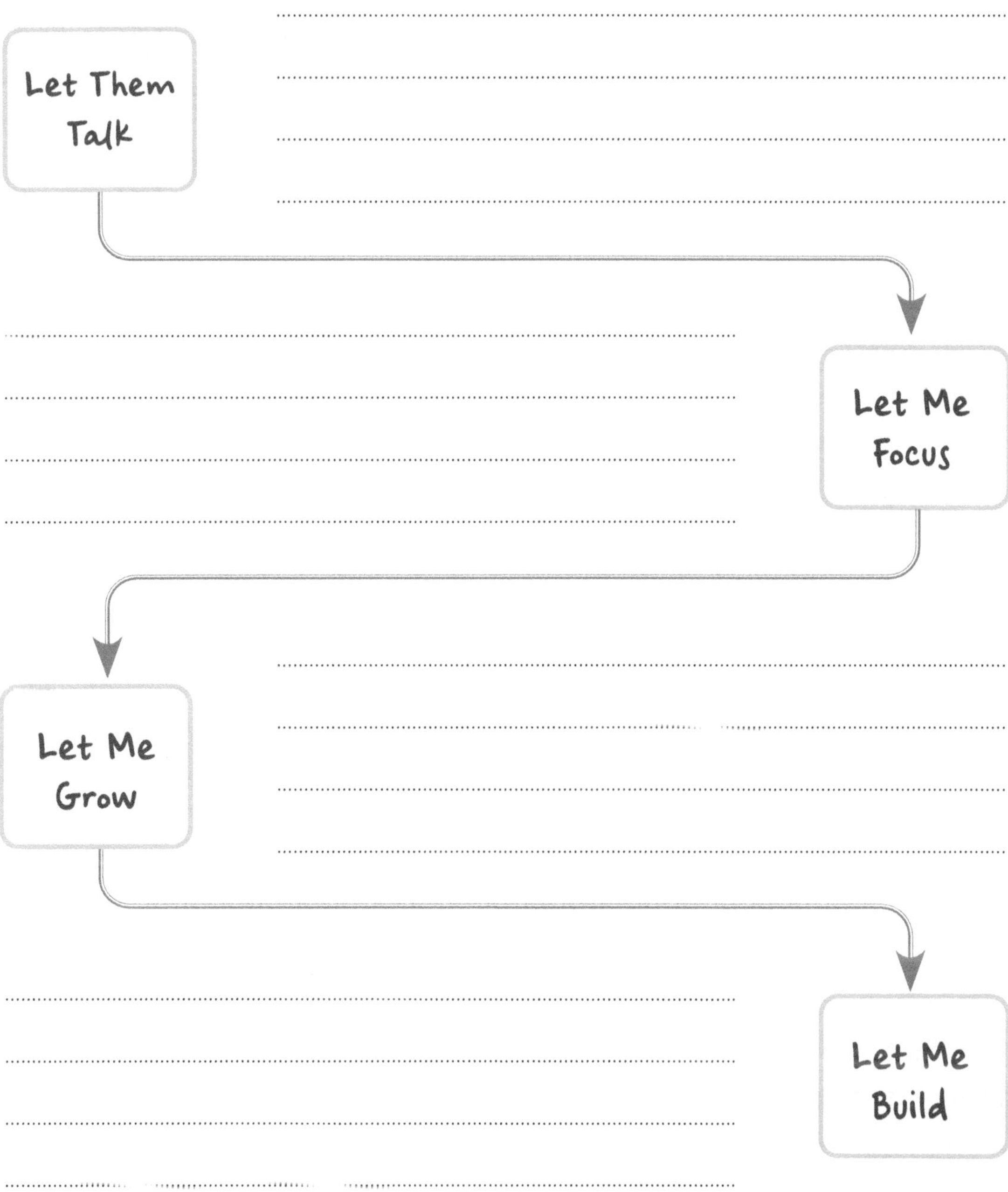

Pro tip: The real power comes from seeing how everything connects. For example, how the "Projection Shield" from Stage 1 supports the "Focus Sanctuary" in Stage 2, which then helps you nurture "Authentic Identity" in Stage 3, finally enabling you to build "Reality Creation" in Stage 4. When you see these connections, you realize these aren't separate techniques but parts of a complete living system.

"I am building a complete living system, not just individual tools."

Day 60: Authentic Living Blueprint

Quick Trigger: "How do I maintain and develop what I've learned?"

Power Question: "How can I design my life to continue living authentically long-term after this program?"

Micro Action: Design *an "Authentic Living Blueprint"* - Create a comprehensive plan for long-term authentic living:

1. Develop a 90-day action plan with:
   - 3-5 specific goals based on your authentic vision
   - Daily/weekly/monthly processes to maintain autonomy
   - Strategies for dealing with challenges and opposition
   - "Don't do" list - behaviors, relationships, or situations that no longer serve your authentic identity
2. Create an "Authentic Living Manifesto" - a short manifesto (1 page) about how you commit to living from now on
3. Set up 30/60/90-day reminder schedules to evaluate and adjust your plan

GOALS – 3–5 AUTHENTIC GOALS FOR 90 DAYS

Goal	Connected to My Vision	Daily/Weekly Habits to Support It	Success Criteria

AUTONOMY ROUTINES – SYSTEMS TO MAINTAIN INNER SOVEREIGNTY

Frequency	Routine / Action	Notes
Daily		
Weekly		
Monthly		

CHALLENGE STRATEGIES – HOW TO RESPOND TO TRIGGERS OR RESISTANCE

Trigger or Challenge	Strategy or Practice to Respond

"DON'T DO" LIST – WHAT NO LONGER SERVES YOUR AUTHENTIC SELF

Behavior	Relationship	Situation to Release

30/60/90-DAY CHECK-IN SCHEDULE

Check-In Day	What to Reflect On	Adjustments to Make
Day 30		
Day 60		
Day 90		

Pro tip: The strongest plan is one that gets implemented. Make sure you include accountability mechanisms in your plan - a buddy partner, support group, coach, or even just a public commitment to yourself on social media or a blog. External accountability can make a huge difference in maintaining your plan when initial enthusiasm fades.

"This is not the end. This is the beginning of my authentic life."

BONUS SECTION: LIFE HARMONY NAVIGATOR (FOR BUSY WOMEN)

Exercise 1: Value-Based Decision Matrix

Quick Trigger: "How can I make quick decisions while staying authentic?"

....

....

....

....

....

Power Question: "What decision-making system can help me balance responsibilities and personal values?"

....

....

....

....

....

....

Micro Action: Create *a "Value-Based Decision Matrix for Busy Women"* - Develop a quick decision tool for busy life:

1. Create a 2x2 matrix with two axes:
   - Vertical axis: "Alignment with core values" (High/Low)
   - Horizontal axis: "Necessity/responsibility level" (High/Low)
2. For each quadrant, develop decision rules:
   - High-High: "Prioritize & Do immediately" (aligns with both values and responsibilities)
   - High-Low: "Schedule intentionally" (aligns with values but not urgent)
   - Low-High: "Simplify & Delegate" (necessary but doesn't align with values)
   - Low-Low: "Decline without apology" (neither necessary nor aligned with values)
3. Create a pocket version of this matrix for daily situations

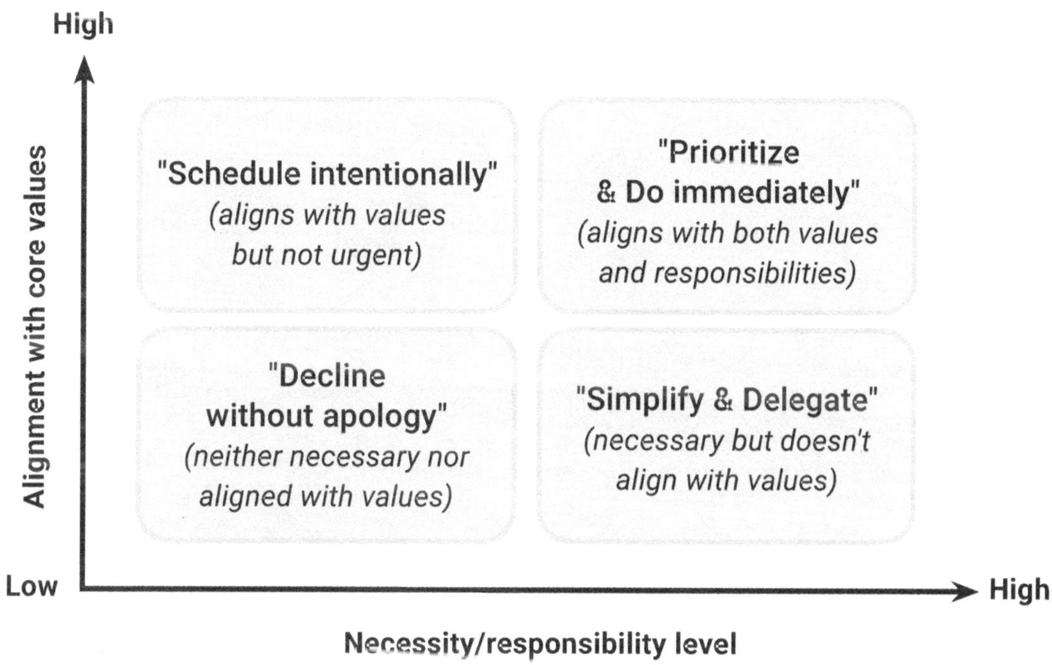

Pro tip: Many busy women feel stuck between responsibilities and personal desires. This matrix doesn't force you to choose one or the other - it helps you categorize decisions so you know how to handle them. Most importantly, recognize that things in the "Low-Low" quadrant are NOT worth your time or energy. True freedom comes from saying "no" to these things.

"I can balance responsibilities and values without sacrificing myself."

Exercise 2: Guilt-Free Boundary Setting

Quick Trigger: "What boundaries do I usually feel guilty about setting?"

....

....

....

....

....

Power Question: "How can I set clear boundaries without feeling guilty or selfish?"

....

....

....

....

....

....

Micro Action: Develop *"Guilt-Free Boundary Setting"* - Create a system for setting boundaries without guilt:

1. Identify 3-5 situations where you usually feel guilty when setting boundaries (declining requests, taking time for yourself, etc.)
2. For each situation, write:
   - Empowering reminder: "When I set this boundary, I am..."
   - 3-part script: Affirmation + Clear boundary + Alternative (if appropriate)
   - Self-care plan: "If I feel guilty, I will..."
3. Create small "guilt-free boundary cards" with reminders and scripts to carry with you

1. ....

Empowering reminder: ....

....

....

3-part script: ....

....

....

....

Self-care plan: ....

....

....

2. ....

Empowering reminder: ....

....

....

3-part script: ....

....

....

....

Self-care plan: ....

....

....

3. ....

Empowering reminder: ....

....

....

3-part script: ....

....

....

....

Self-care plan: ....

....

....

4. ....

Empowering reminder: ....

....

....

3-part script: ....

....

....

....

Self-care plan: ....

....

....

5. ....

Empowering reminder: ....

....

....

3-part script: ....

....

....

....

Self-care plan: ....

....

....

Pro tip: One of the biggest culprits causing guilt when setting boundaries is using long reasons or apologies. Contrary to intuition, short, clear, and confident boundaries often receive less pushback and create less guilt. Instead of saying "I'm so sorry, I wish I could help, but...", try "I can't take on additional work right now" or "I'm focusing on X this week, so I won't be available for Y."

"My boundaries aren't about rejecting others but about respecting myself."

Final Milestone

CONGRATULATIONS! You've completed the entire 60-day journey!

Take a moment to truly immerse yourself in this amazing achievement. You've done deep work that most people never have the courage to undertake. You've faced the fear of being judged, protected your focus, redefined your authentic identity, and now, you're proactively building a life on YOUR terms.

To mark this milestone, complete the following sentence and record it in your journal:

"After 60 days, I have freed ___ mental energy, abandoned ________________ limiting identities, and am building ______________ based on my authentic identity."

Example: "After 60 days, I have freed 70% of the mental energy previously spent worrying about others' opinions, abandoned the limiting identity of 'people pleaser,' and am building a career that reflects my creativity and freedom based on my authentic identity."

This journey isn't about reaching a fixed destination - it's about learning to live YOUR life every day. You now have the tools and strategies to continue this journey for years to come.

Remember: "While others sit in the stands judging, you can continue building in the arena. They may exhaust themselves with judgment; you will thrive with building."

Share your journey: If you feel comfortable, share your full 60-day journey on social media using the hashtag #LetThemTalkLetMeBuild. Magic happens when we not only live authentically but also inspire others to do the same.

ONE LAST THING BEFORE YOU GO...

Your Review Can Change Someone's Life

Dear friend,

You've just completed (or are about to complete) a transformative 60-day journey. You've learned to free yourself from the need for approval, built your focus sanctuary, redefined your authentic self, and begun creating life on your own terms.

Now, I have a small favor to ask.

Would You Share Your Experience?

If this book has made a difference in your life - even a small one - would you consider leaving a review on Amazon?

Here's why it matters:

- **Your review helps others find this book.** In a sea of self-help promises, your honest experience helps someone like you discover a path that actually works.
- **Your story inspires courage.** When someone reads that you've successfully completed the journey, they think: "If they can do it, maybe I can too."
- **Your feedback helps me serve better.** I read every review and use your insights to improve future editions and create better resources.

How to Leave a Review:

1. Go to the book's Amazon page
2. Click "Write a customer review"
3. Share your honest experience - *what worked, what challenged you, what changed*

Not Sure What to Write?

Consider sharing:

- Which stage impacted you most and why
- One specific change you've noticed in your life
- Who you would recommend this book to
- Your favorite tool or exercise from the journey

Even a brief review makes a huge difference. A simple "This book helped me stop caring so much about others' opinions and start building my own life" can be the nudge someone needs to begin their transformation.

Thank You for Being Part of This Movement

Every person who completes this journey makes the "Let Them Talk, Let Me Build" community stronger. Your review isn't just feedback - it's a beacon for others seeking the same freedom you've found.

Thank you for trusting me with your 60 days. Thank you for doing the work. And thank you, in advance, for helping others find their path.

"While they exhaust themselves judging, we'll be busy building - together."

With gratitude and respect,

Addison Gray

Made in United States
Cleveland, OH
14 August 2025

19407803R00111